THE THINKING CLASSROOM

Supporting educators to embed critical and creative thinking

Alice Vigors

Copyright © Alice Vigors 2022

All rights reserved. No part of this book may be reproduced or transmitted in any form or by any means, electronic or mechanical, including photocopying, recording or by any information storage and retrieval system, without prior permission in writing from the publisher.

Published by Amba Press
Melbourne, Australia
www.ambapress.com.au

Editor – Rica Dearman
Cover designer – Tess McCabe

ISBN: 9781922607348 (pbk)
ISBN: 9781922607355 (ebk)

A catalogue record for this book is available from the National Library of Australia.

*To my husband, Ben,
and my three beautiful children,
Miles, Norah and Stella.*

Praise for *The Thinking Classroom*

The Thinking Classroom does what few books have accomplished before: it guides educators in creating learning experiences that cultivate critical and creative thinking in their scholars. Alice Vigors walks readers through how to help students understand themselves better as learners and to be more reflective and aware of their own thinking. Through a personable and informed lens, readers are offered a comprehensive overview of what it means to nurture future-ready learners. I am certain *The Thinking Classroom* will be a highly referenced book in my inquiry repertoire.

Trevor McKenzie, teacher and author of the bestselling books Dive into Inquiry and the Inquiry Mindset series

The Thinking Classroom was astutely written by Alice with so many great insights and examples of quality practice. The practical nature of this book means teachers can implement ideas in their classroom straight away. I absolutely loved reading this book.

Aaron Johnston, assistant principal and founder of Mr J's Learning Space

The Thinking Classroom is a must-have for all educators. Alice clearly and authentically articulates with an abundance of practical resources how critical and creative thinking is integral to student success.

James Gray, deputy principal

I love the practical nature of this book. The fact that you can scan a QR code to locate additional information and resources is brilliant. *The Thinking Classroom* is a must-read for every teacher and leader.

Rebecca West, deputy principal and founder of Talkin' Chalk

The Thinking Classroom is a very easy-to-read book with so many practical strategies I could apply in my classroom tomorrow. There were so many 'ah-ha' moments in this book and powerful statements that really helped me to see the link between my current classroom practice and the fostering of a thinking classroom. A definite must-read.

Demetra Vekic, classroom teacher

About the author

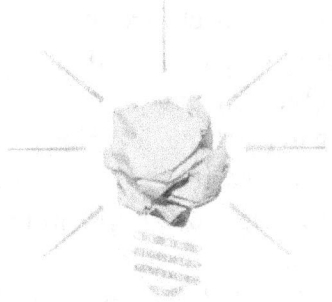

Alice Vigors is a dedicated and passionate assistant principal: curriculum and instruction, who uses her creativity, innovation and dedication to inspire others and build their capacity to make a positive difference to the education of all students. She has been a teacher and leader for more than 13 years, working in both the NSW Public and Catholic education systems. She holds three degrees from the University of Newcastle, including a Bachelor of Teaching/Bachelor of Arts (double degree), Graduate Certificate in Theology and a Master of Educational Studies with distinction.

You might be surprised to learn that teaching was not Alice's first choice when trying to decide on the nine choices to submit to the Universities Admissions Centre (UAC) at the end of Year 12 – meteorology was. When the Universities Admission Index (UAI) was released, Alice was devastated to learn she didn't have the score to do meteorology, but after many tears, words of wisdom from her mother steered her in the direction of teaching and the rest, they say, is history. When deciding to become a teacher, Alice knew that she wanted to be like the teachers who inspired and challenged her to be the best learner she could possibly be, Mrs Toby and Mr Vane Tempest. They saw Alice's passions and talents and utilised those to help her to be a successful learner. Alice also draws on a teacher that had a negative impact on her, recalling her Year 5 teacher who taught her the effect and impact of putting someone down and telling them they'll never 'get' something in Mathematics. Lucky for her, Alice is the type of person who uses this as fuel for the fire and she set out to prove her wrong.

Alice has developed a website, blog and professional learning network called 'Thinking Pathways', a resource and information hub for sharing her knowledge and examples of classroom practice around the explicit teaching and scaffolding of critical and creative thinking skills, the implementation of visible learning practices and understanding the role of inquiry learning in teaching, learning and leading. She delivers high-quality professional learning, by invitation, to teachers and leaders both in face-to-face workshops around NSW and virtually to educators globally. Alice launched and co-hosts an educational podcast in March 2021 called the 'Teacher Takeaway' to provide educators with practical takeaway ideas across a range of educational topics with three other prominent educational leaders, which made the top 100 Australian podcasts in the first nine months.

Acknowledgements

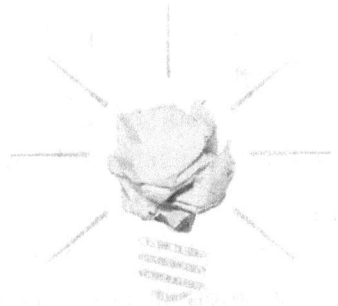

To achieve great things, it takes a village. I would like to take this opportunity to thank my village who have helped make this dream of mine a reality.

Firstly, to my husband, Ben, thank you for always supporting me and encouraging me to pursue my dreams. This journey would not be the same without you by my side every step of the way. I am grateful for your levelheadedness. You keep me grounded.

To my three beautiful children, Miles, Norah and Stella. This world is full of wonderful things and great opportunities if you work hard and persist with what you are working towards. I hope that I cannot just teach you but show you through my actions that anything is possible if you dare to dream.

To my parents, Julianne and Matthew, thank you for showing me the value of hard work, persistence and dedication. Your encouragement and words of wisdom helped me to dream big and made me realise I could truly achieve anything I put my mind to.

To my siblings and my friends, who were patient with me as I chased after jobs that moved me across the state, developed a website, co-hosted a podcast and wrote this book. Even though at times we might be separated by distance, your calls and chats give me the distraction I need to recharge and refocus.

To my colleagues, Donna and the TPS teaching family; Gary and the OLR teaching families. Thank you for your ongoing support, kindness and friendship. I am truly lucky to work alongside an amazing group of educators and feel blessed to have made some lifelong friends. A special thank you to Donna and Gary, whose guidance and leadership showed me what true leadership is all about.

To the Teacher Takeaway podcast team. Thank you for being my sounding board and talking through my ideas with me. The work you do, Bec, Aaron and James, to support educators from all sectors is truly inspiring and I am so grateful I can lead and learn alongside you.

To the man who became the catalyst for change in my teaching and leadership approach, Dr Ron Ritchhart. Your work inspired me to create a better educational experience for not only the students in my class, but for all of the students around me. Thank you for paving the way in education and providing a guiding light for so many educators.

To my publisher, Alicia, from Amba Press. Thank you for seeing potential in my writing and helping me to create my vision. You challenged me to write this book and I thank you for pushing and guiding me.

Finally, to educators everywhere, thank you for choosing to shape the future through the incredibly important work you do each day with your students. It is an exciting time to be an educator, and I am so thankful to each and every one of you who has chosen to join me on this journey.

Table of contents

About the author		vii
Acknowledgements		ix
Introduction		1
Part one	**The role of critical and creative thinking**	**7**
Chapter 1	What is critical and creative thinking?	7
Chapter 2	Why is critical and creative thinking important in the classroom?	21
Part two	**Pedagogy and planning for thinking**	**35**
Chapter 3	Explicit teaching, visible learning and the gradual release of responsibility	35

| Chapter 4 | Thinking routines and the art of questioning | 51 |
| Chapter 5 | Planning for critical and creative thinking in the classroom | 65 |

Part three **The thinking classroom in action** **81**
Chapter 6	Critical and creative thinking in literacy	81
Chapter 7	Critical and creative thinking in numeracy	101
Chapter 8	Critical and creative thinking in other key learning areas	121
Chapter 9	Feedback and self-reflection	141

Part four **Assessing student thinking** **159**
Chapter 10	How do we assess students' thinking?	159
Chapter 11	How do we assess students' depth of understanding?	173
Chapter 12	How do we utilise the SOLO Taxonomy to shift student thinking?	183

Part five **Leading teams in critical and creative thinking** **195**
| Chapter 13 | How do I support my team to embed critical and creative thinking in their practice? | 195 |

Conclusion	209
List of figures	217
List of tables	220
References	221

Introduction

*"Critical thinking narrows and
creative thinking expands,
but they must work in tandem for
problem-solving and decision-making"*

Pearl Zhu

Critical and creative thinking are often labelled as 'soft' skills and considered by many as buzz words in the Australian education system; however, these seemingly 'soft' skills provide the foundation from which students learn to build an understanding of different concepts across and between subject areas, as well as support them as they learn to make sense of the world around them. In Australian schools, critical and creative thinking are classified as general capabilities, which means that they permeate all learning areas and underpin the development of content knowledge and skills across the curriculum. In a rapidly evolving world that values the thinking capabilities of people, it is important that educators don't just leave the development of student thinking to chance, but ensure that it is strategically planned, designed, modelled, scaffolded and assessed in order to move learning forward and achieve the best educational outcomes for all students.

This book was written with the teacher and leader in mind and is a mix of foundational theory and practical strategies and tools you can take away and apply in your classroom or with your teams tomorrow. It is divided into five parts, with each component diving into key areas of embedding critical and creative thinking into practice.

Part one

The role of critical and creative thinking examines the role of critical and creative thinking in the Australian schooling system and outlines reasons why these 'soft' skills are crucial for all students to master. It is therefore paramount that educators have a strong understanding of what critical and creative thinking entail, the differences between the two and how they intersect each other. Educators will examine the Australian Curriculum, Assessment and Reporting Authority (ACARA) learning continuum and explore the four key components of it in order to understand how the development of thinking progresses as students move through their schooling. By the end of part one, educators will be able to:

- Understand why metacognition is important
- Understand the difference between critical and creative thinking
- Elaborate on the connections between the two types of thinking
- Examine the role of critical and creative thinking in the classroom setting

- Understand the ACARA Critical and Creative Thinking learning continuum
- Reflect on and explore the implications on their own classroom practice

Part two

Pedagogy and planning for thinking dives deeper into the pedagogical practices that support the development of critical and creative thinking skills in the classroom and highlights ways teachers can explicitly plan for and structure thinking to enhance the metacognitive processes of their students. Educators will unpack ways that evidence-based practices such as explicit instruction and visible learning combined with thinking routines and effective questioning can be leveraged in every classroom to support and enhance the thought processes of students. Educators will also be provided with practical tips and strategies for planning for and implementing these pedagogical practices in their teaching practice. By the end of part two, educators will be able to:

- Explain the pedagogical practices that support critical and creative thinking
- Identify strategies that can be employed in their teaching practice
- Understand the role of explicit instruction in scaffolding thinking moves for students
- Explain the role of thinking routines in supporting metacognition
- Understand the phases of development and their implications on the development of student thinking in the classroom
- Identify the role of questioning in the classroom
- Utilise the Australian Professional Standards for Teachers in the planning cycle
- Understand ways to plan for critical and creative thinking

Part three

The thinking classroom in action highlights practical examples of thinking routines in action in the classroom setting. Its aim is to support teacher understanding of how thinking routines can be utilised across the curriculum to scaffold the development of, deepen and assess student thinking and level of understanding. Educators will be introduced to a number of thinking routines, their purpose and be provided with practical examples of how I have utilised them in my own practice, including snapshots of student learning samples and QR code links to the Thinking Pathways website where educators can explore templates and videos of educators applying the thinking routine. Educators will explore the importance of providing feedback to students about their thinking and examine ways they can leverage self-reflection to support student growth and awareness of their thought processes. By the end of part three, educators will be able to:

- Identify a range of thinking routines
- Explain how thinking routines support and scaffold student thinking in literacy
- Explain how thinking routines support and scaffold student thinking in numeracy
- Explain how thinking routines support and scaffold student thinking in other key learning areas
- Understand the role of feedback and self-reflection in the development of thinking
- Explain how reflective thinking routines support and scaffold a student's ability to think about and reflect upon their thinking
- Reflect on and explore the implications on their own classroom practice

Part four
Assessing student thinking unpacks the role of assessment and how educators can utilise thinking tools, such as thinking routines, to ascertain the level of student thinking and how to move thinking forward in order for students to develop a deeper understanding of concepts and content, and be able to apply this understanding to a range of different situations and subject areas. Educators will explore the notion of surface, deep and transfer learning, and develop an understanding about why all three levels are important for students' learning growth and development. Through developing a deeper understanding of the levels of learning and how they intersect with the phases of thinking development, educators will examine the SOLO Taxonomy and explore ways they can leverage this to pinpoint student

understanding and identify ways to move learning and understanding forward. By the end of part four, educators will be able to:

- Understand the role of assessment in the development of student thinking
- Identify ways we can leverage thinking routines as part of the assessment process
- Identify the key components of the three phases of learning: surface, deep and transfer
- Explain ways to assess the depth of understanding and critical and creative thinking skills through the three phases of learning
- Understand the range of levels in the SOLO Taxonomy model
- Explain how the SOLO model can be used to support critical and creative thinking in the classroom

Part five

Leading teams in critical and creative thinking explores ways that educators who lead a team of teachers can utilise the principles and practices that underpin critical and creative thinking to support and build the capacity of their team to effectively implement and build these skills in their students. Educators will explore the Action Research or action inquiry model and the role of collaboration in this process to support the building and sustainability of classrooms that have a strong critical and creative thinking culture. Educators will understand how they can utilise thinking routines to support the process of analysing data and student learning samples in order to make informed and consistent judgements about the level of student thinking and depth of understanding across classes, grades and stages. By the end of part five, educators will be able to:

- Understand the need to develop an action inquiry/research process with their team
- Explain the role of collaboration in collectively building a culture of critical and creative thinking
- Identify how thinking routines can be used to examine and analyse data and student learning samples

PART ONE

THE ROLE OF CRITICAL AND CREATIVE THINKING

CHAPTER 1

What is critical and creative thinking?

When you tell someone you are thinking, what is actually going on in your head?

How many times have you actually stopped to think about the answer to this question? I'm guessing it's not really something you have given much thought to before now. This was certainly the case for me when Ron Ritchhart posed this question to a room full of educational leaders and teachers at a professional learning seminar back in 2017. I hadn't stopped to think about what I do when I think and therefore probably wasn't clear in providing clarity to my students about what it might look like, sound like and feel like prior to this moment. This moment changed my teaching forever. It became the catalyst for a shift in my pedagogical practice. If we, as educators, are not clear about our own thought processes and have a good understanding of the types of thinking we do, then how will we be able to effectively make our thinking visible to others and support our students to do the same?

This chapter will explore the research surrounding the capability of critical and creative thinking, and seeks to provide a common definition to build your understanding of the differences between the two kinds of thinking as well as their intersecting characteristics. It will unpack why metacognition is important for a thriving society, examining the implications for teachers in the classroom.

Chapter learning intentions

By the end of this chapter, educators will be able to:

- Understand why metacognition is important
- Understand the difference between critical and creative thinking
- Elaborate on the connections between the two types of thinking

Unpacking metacognition

The term 'metacognition' is used to describe thinking about an individual's cognitive processes and activity. Simply put, it is the process of 'thinking about thinking' (Ritchhart, Church & Morrison, 2011; Lamb, Maire & Doecke, 2017). Frequently, it is subsumed under the broader notion of 'self-regulated learning' and is associated with improved learning and academic outcomes. Metacognition includes being able to recognise the processes we use when we think about something, as well as recognising when we don't know something yet.

This ability is, of course, mediated by the age of the learner; however, this doesn't mean that our youngest students cannot begin to 'think about their thinking'. Younger children have more of a limited capacity to undertake metacognitive processes than older children, but limited doesn't mean they cannot do it at all, as highlighted by Frey et al (2018). It simply means that instructional routines are required to prompt self-questioning in order to support this (Frey, Hattie & Fisher, 2018). Metacognition is seen as involving both knowledge about cognitive processes and strategies for monitoring these processes with research highlighting that the development of student metacognition is best engaged through specific curriculum areas, since metacognitive skills depend on both content knowledge and expertise (Lamb, Maire & Doecke, 2017).

Implications for the classroom

As our society evolves, the need for our students to be active thinkers becomes more apparent. Reflections on the knowledge and skills students must acquire in education for future success and wellbeing is certainly not a new concept (Lamb, Maire & Doecke, 2017). As educators, it is our job to ensure that our students are equipped with the necessary skills to move beyond superficial and surface-level thinking to more advanced and higher-order thinking that includes critical and creative thinking. This is not to say that surface-level thinking doesn't have a place in the classroom – quite the opposite. Surface-level thinking and learning experiences are important components of the learning process and are essential building blocks to the development of deep understanding. This notion will be covered further in part four.

Thinking is the mental process of using information to reach a conclusion. For students to be highly effective thinkers, they must be presented with structures and frameworks that can assist them in being more proficient at the act of thinking. Generally speaking, the process of thinking involves our ability to take in and make sense of information as it is presented to us in multiple ways. A proficient thinker is able to then connect, apply and transform this information into unique and novel ideas, drawing on their capacity to critically analyse, evaluate and problem-solve in order to synthesise ideas and generate creative solutions (Cash, 2011).

Our students must be equipped to think differently, cogently and flexibly to thrive in today's world. The challenges of today's society require young people to be creative, innovative, enterprising and adaptable, with the motivation, confidence and skills to use critical and creative thinking purposefully.

I'd like to pose this question to you now: *When you tell someone you are thinking, what is actually going on in your head?* Take a moment to really think about what this looks and feels like for you as a learner before engaging with the activity below.

Activity: What goes on in your head when you're thinking?

Brainstorm a list of things you do when you are thinking. For example, wondering.

The critical and creative thinking capability combines two types of thinking:

1. Critical thinking, and
2. Creative thinking

Though the two are not interchangeable, they are strongly linked, bringing complementary dimensions to the thinking and learning process (Australian Curriculum, Assessment and Reporting Authority, n.d.).

Before we jump into defining these two types of thinking, let's take a moment to engage with the thinking routine Generate, Sort, Connect, Elaborate (Ritchhart, Church & Morrison, 2011) to help us understand key skills and connections between critical and creative thinking. This thinking routine is perfect for helping us to examine generated ideas and draw connections between ideas.

Activity: Generate, Sort, Connect, Elaborate thinking routine

Step 1: Examine the following *generated* list of skills:

Thinking we do when we generate ideas	Pose questions	Thinking we do when we judge ideas
Imagine possibilities	Consider perspectives	Brainstorm solutions
Identify pros and cons	Elaborate	Cause and effect
Improvise	Consider alternatives	Speculate
Draw conclusions	Use intuition	Reason with evidence
Curiosity	Imagination	

Step 2: *Sort* these skills on the following page into skills you think are required for critical thinking and those required for creative thinking.

Step 3: *Connect* ideas and skills that you know have something in common or are related/linked to each other by drawing connecting lines from one to the other.

Step 4: *Elaborate* on these connections by writing a short explanation about how or why you think these skills are connected.

Scan the QR code to find out more about the Generate, Sort, Connect, Elaborate thinking routine.

GCSE activity page:

Below is an example of a worked GCSE concept map. This example highlights some of the connections that educators have drawn to different critical and creative thinking skills. What is evident when you first examine this example are the numerous lines travelling between and across ideas. This highlights the notion that while critical and creative thinking have core skills and processes, they are often intersecting and draw on each other when one is looking to problem-solve and develop a product of learning.

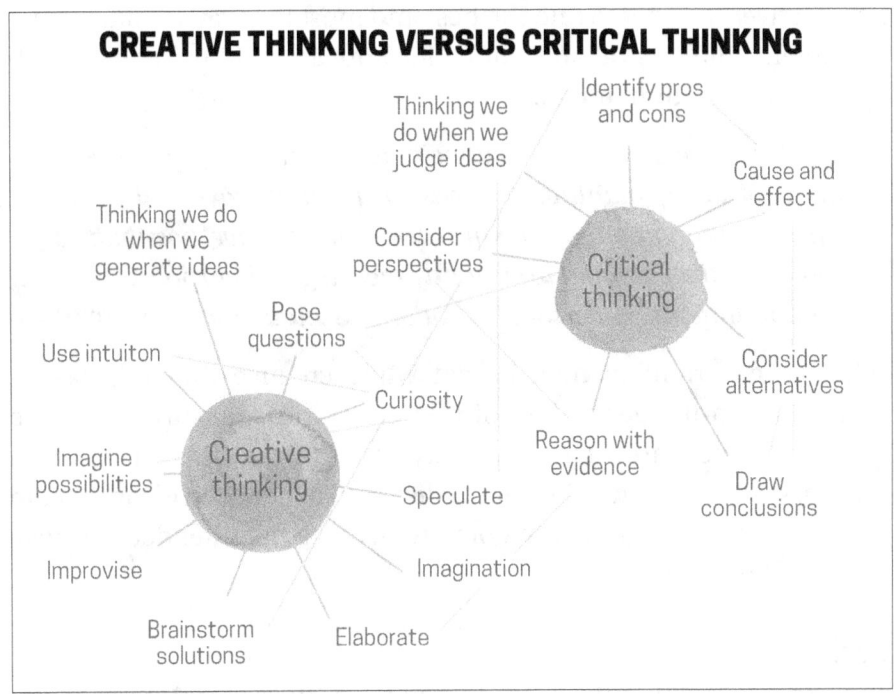

Figure 1: GCSE concept map brainstorm example

For example:

The creative thinking skill of brainstorming solutions is often undertaken in parallel with the critical thinking skill of identifying pros and cons. While they both require an individual to think about and approach something in a particular way, the connection they share is the identification of possibilities and the ability to examine things from a range of perspectives.

What is creative thinking?

Creative thinking, in its simplest form, is the ability to make something new. The mental process of thinking creatively requires students to draw on their imagination, using their skills to combine, change, reshape, refine or improve ideas and solutions (Cash, 2011). Creative thinking is, at its core, a generative process that focuses on the number of ideas as well as the range of ideas generated. It relies on one's ability to manipulate and play around with ideas, looking from a range of perspectives in order to find the best and most innovative solution for a problem. The Australian Council for Educational Research (ACER) defines creative thinking as:

> *"To think creatively is the capacity to generate many different kinds of ideas, manipulate ideas in unusual ways and make unconventional connections in order to outline novel possibilities that have the potential to elegantly meet a given purpose."*
> *(Ramalingam, Anderson, Duckworth, Scoular & Heard, 2020)*

What is important to note is that while creative thinking has its foundation in the generation of numerous ideas, ensuring that the ideas generated are of high quality is important. In a classroom setting, students need to be able to distinguish between ideas that are 'good' and those that are not going to achieve the intended purpose or desired outcome.

Goal:
The goal of creative thinking, therefore, is to explore many ideas, generate several possibilities and look for many 'right' answers. Critical thinking plays a crucial role in a student's ability to problem-solve.

Examples of creative thinking skills:
In the classroom, there are a number of verbs that teachers use that draw on creative thinking skills, including:

- Brainstorming (brain . storm)
  To solve a problem or come up with ideas
- Elaborating (elab . o . rate)
  To expand on something in detail

- Imagining (imag . ine)
  To form a mental image of something
- Questioning (ques . tion)
  To ask questions in order to seek information
- Improvising (im . pro . vise)
  To make, invent or arrange something out of what is conveniently on hand
- Speculating (spec . u . late)
  To review something and ponder on it
- Drawing (draw)
  To cause attention to be given to someone or something
- Creating (cre . ate)
  To make or produce something

While this is by no means an exhaustive list, it provides a clear snapshot for educators about some of the tasks that require students to draw upon their creative thinking skills and what that type of thinking is requiring our students to do. For example, imagining requires our students to form a mental picture of something by piecing together snippets of information to form a larger picture. This type of thinking also asks our students to draw on their understanding and prior knowledge of a broad range of areas to make sense of something. Some of our students find this an easy task to perform, while others find it a little more challenging.

What is critical thinking?

The notion of critical thinking is not a new one. In fact, people have been referring to critical thinking for decades and as such there is an abundance of definitions and research out there. In many ways, critical thinking is often considered the opposite of creative thinking. Whereas creative thinking is more intuitive, is shaped somewhat randomly and seeks multiple answers, critical thinking is more ordered, directed and controlled. Both types of thinking, however, require advanced levels of brain energy and seek to generate reasoned solutions.

Critical thinking is about developing autonomous thinkers. For educators, this means we want students to be independent and self-directed learners who can identify, evaluate and reason with evidence in a broader context beyond themselves. ACER defines critical thinking as:

> *"To think critically is to analyse and evaluate information, reasoning and situations, according to appropriate standards, for the purpose of constructing sound and insightful new knowledge, understandings, hypotheses and beliefs. Critical thinking encompasses the subject's ability to process and synthesise information in such a way that it enables them to apply it judiciously to tasks for informed decision-making and effective problem-solving."*
> (Heard, Scoular, Duckworth, Ramalingam & Teo, 2020)

Critical thinking is at the core of most intellectual activity and involves students learning to recognise or develop an argument, use evidence in support of that argument, draw reasoned conclusions and use information to solve problems.

Goal:

The goal, therefore, of critical thinking is to arrive at one conclusion and make good decisions based on evidence and facts. It is the thinking that we do when we make judgements about ideas.

Examples of critical thinking skills:

In the classroom, there are a number of verbs that teachers use that draw on critical thinking skills, including:

- Interpreting (in . ter . pret)
  To explain the meaning of something
  To understand something in a specific way
- Analysing (an . a . lyse)
  To study something closely and carefully
- Evaluating (eval . u . ate)
  To judge the value or condition of something in a careful and thoughtful way
- Explaining (ex . plain)
  To make something clear or easy to understand

- Sequencing (se . quence)
  To arrange in a sequence
- Reasoning (rea . son)
  To make a statement or fact that explains why something is the way it is
- Comparing (com . pare)
  To say that something is similar to something else
- Questioning (ques . tion)
  To ask questions in order to seek information
- Inferring (in . fer)
  To draw conclusions from facts or a premise
- Hypothesising (hy . poth . e . sise)
  To make an assumption or theory that is not proven, but that leads to further study or discussion
- Appraising (ap . praise)
  To make or express a critical judgement or evaluation
- Testing (test)
  To put an idea or theory to the test in order to prove something
- Generalising (gen . er . al . ise)
  To make a general statement or draw a general conclusion

Understanding the kind of thinking you are asking students to undertake means that you can be clear in your instruction about what that type of thinking looks like, employ the most appropriate structure and scaffold to support students through the metacognitive process and provide clarity and feedback on how that type of thinking is demonstrated through a product of learning. It is in this space that the rest of this book seeks to offer advice and support to educators of all experience levels.

Are they really connected?

When we examine the ACER definitions of both critical and creative thinking, it is clear that there are distinct differences, yet when we refer to and talk about thinking skills, we discuss them in association with one another. Critical thinking and creative thinking are described as complementary and similar, but they are not identical processes

(Halpern, 2003). Lamb et al (2017) highlights that the Australian Curriculum, for example, acknowledges the strong link between them through the general capability of 'critical and creative thinking'. Other states and territories around Australia have followed suit, embedding the general capability of critical and creative thinking across their syllabus documents.

In the analytical report *Key Skills for the 21st Century: An Evidence-Based Review*, Lamb and his colleagues point out that critical thinking is often seen as a condition for creativity and vice versa (2017). Both critical and creative thinking require more than a technical set of skills. Important dispositions and related skills underpin a student's ability to think critically as well as creatively, drawing on other related cognitive abilities such as problem-solving, problem identification and idea generation.

> "Creative and critical thinking are two sides of the same coin: One is of little use without the other."
>
> (Alghafri & Ismail, 2014)

When we think about critical and creative thinking as two sides of the same coin, we can begin to notice how the two types of thinking interplay and interconnect with each other. For example, if we examine generative and evaluative thought processes, we notice that the creative thinking skill of generating ideas requires a person to think of and brainstorm multiple ideas from different angles and perspectives, whereas the critical thinking skill of evaluation requires a person to examine the merit and value of something, often looking at the pros and cons. While they require a different way of thinking, generative and evaluative thought processes often go hand in hand. In the classroom this might look like:

- Asking students to brainstorm ideas
- Asking students to decide which is the best idea
- Asking students to evaluate why this idea is the best one to choose
- Asking students to explain their judgements

Understanding the interconnected nature of critical and creative thinking is essential as we move towards recognising how we can embed metacognitive thinking processes into our classrooms.

Chapter reflection questions

After reading chapter 1, take a moment to reflect on your learning and understanding.

1. Why do you think metacognition is important to the work of all teachers?
2. Reflect on your responses to the two learning activities in this chapter.
   a. What do you notice about the way you responded?
   b. Did you include more critical thinking skills than creative thinking skills during your brainstorm? What makes you say that?
3. Think about a lesson or unit of work you have recently taught. Reflect on and describe:
   a. Opportunities where students were asked to use and apply critical thinking.
   b. Opportunities where students were asked to use and apply creative thinking.
   c. How did you support the development of these thought processes?
   d. Were there times when these were just left up to chance? Why might this be?

CHAPTER 2

Why is critical and creative thinking important in the classroom?

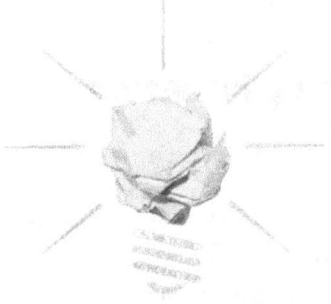

"The principal goal of education is to create people who are capable of doing new things, not simply of repeating what other generations have done"

Jean Piaget, cognitive psychologist

Over the years, there has been a growing number of calls for education to have a renewed focus on higher-order thinking skills and capabilities, which are often referred to as '21st-century skills' or 'soft skills'. If you read any article, blog or report that is connected to this term, you will notice that it is these skills that employers believe are necessary to prepare our students for an increasingly complex world (Ellerton, 2017). Many syllabus and curriculum documents around Australia recognise this, and as such have embedded these '21st-century skills and capabilities' into and across the curriculum, including critical and creative thinking.

This chapter explores the role of critical and creative thinking in today's classroom, looking specifically at how this capability is aligned to the New South Wales and Australian Curriculums. It will unpack the ACARA Critical and Creative Thinking learning continuum, examining the goal and purpose of the four distinct elements. This chapter will also explore how educators can utilise critical and creative thinking to enhance the application of knowledge, skills and understanding of our students in the classroom.

Chapter learning intentions

By the end of this chapter, educators will be able to:

- Examine the role of critical and creative thinking in the classroom setting
- Understand the ACARA Critical and Creative Thinking learning continuum
- Reflect on and explore the implications on their own classroom practice

Education researchers, policymakers and private enterprise all agree that, in addition to content knowledge, students in the 21st century need to acquire particular skills to equip them for a modern world, one of which is the ability to think – and think well. It is therefore no surprise that critical thinking, creativity, metacognition, problem-solving and collaboration are some of the 21st-century skills that receive the most attention from policymakers, researchers and practitioners, in any discussion related to 21st-century skills (Drabsch, 2019).

The Australian Curriculum, NSW Syllabus and the syllabus documents of many of the other states and territories around Australia recognise the importance of building these capabilities in our students, through including critical and creative thinking as a general capability across the curriculum or syllabus documents. These curriculums are detailed and articulate clearly the critical and creative thinking skills that a child needs to develop as they progress through school. How and where these skills are taught remains solely the decision of the school and the teachers in its classrooms (Hughes, 2015).

Being an effective practitioner requires a teacher to know the content and how to teach it, which means teachers need to be able to clearly identify and articulate learning that draws on the skills of critical and creative thinking. Teachers also need to be able to explicitly scaffold the metacognitive process in order to support students to think about, manipulate and generate ideas and solutions, and reflect on how their thinking has grown over time. It is not enough, however, for teachers to simply scaffold thinking. Students need to be able to apply critical and creative thinking skills on something for which they need certain content knowledge.

A lack of content knowledge significantly hinders the expression of critical and creative thinking skills (Lamb, Maire & Doecke, 2017). It is therefore essential that teachers use the curriculum content as the vehicle and foundation on which to foster a student's metacognitive processes. There is also the matter of context dependence. This simply means that a student may be able to apply or employ a particular kind of thinking in one subject area but struggle to do the same in another subject area. This highlights, again, the importance of strong content knowledge along with the provision of opportunities to transfer our learning across curriculum disciplines.

As educators, we want students to become proficient with the kinds of thinking they can use to develop their own understanding of things. In the book *Making Thinking Visible*, Ron Ritchhart and colleagues (2011) highlight that we want the students in our schools to be able to:

- Ask questions, identify puzzles and wonder about the mysteries and implications of the objects and ideas of learning.
- Make connections, comparisons and contrasts between and among things – including connections within and across the discipline, as well as with one's own prior knowledge.
- Build ongoing and evolving explanations, interpretations and theories based on one's ever-developing knowledge and understanding.
- Examine things from different perspectives and alternative points of view to discern bias and develop a more balanced take on issues, ideas and events.
- Notice, observe and look closely to fully perceive details, nuances and hidden aspects and to observe what is really going on as the foundational evidence for one's interpretations and theories.
- Identify, gather and reason with evidence to justify and support one's interpretations, predictions, theories, arguments and explanations.
- Delve deeper to uncover the complexities and challenges of a topic and look below the surface of things, recognising when one has only a surface understanding.
- Be able to capture the core or essence of a thing to discern what it is really all about.

The 2008 *Melbourne Declaration on Educational Goals for Young Australians* recognises that the skills of critical and creative thinking are fundamental to the success of all students in our schools. Through utilising a clear sequence of thinking skills and applying 'thinking moves' or routines, educators are best placed to support the development of students' metacognitive processes. The ACARA supports this notion with the development of the Critical and Creative Thinking learning continuum. This continuum of thinking skills highlights for educators how a student's metacognitive processes or thinking skills should develop as they move through their schooling from Kindergarten or Foundation through to Year 10. McGuinness (1999) highlights that embedding thinking skills in the classroom to support the development of content knowledge, understanding and skills is fundamental in supporting active cognitive processing, which goes hand in hand with strong student achievement.

ACARA Critical and Creative Thinking learning continuum

The ACARA Critical and Creative Thinking learning continuum is separated into the following four distinct elements that contribute to the demonstration of critical and creative thinking:

1. Inquiring: identifying, exploring and organising information and ideas
2. Generating ideas, possibilities and actions
3. Analysing, synthesising and evaluating reasoning and procedures
4. Reflecting on thinking and processes

These four elements are not a cyclical set nor are they linear in nature. Rather, they are four interrelated elements that each contribute to the metacognitive processes one uses when they engage in the learning process. With this in mind, it is important that educators are providing students with opportunities to develop them explicitly and simultaneously, in order to build and foster critical and creative thinkers (Australian Curriculum, Assessment and Reporting Authority, n.d.).

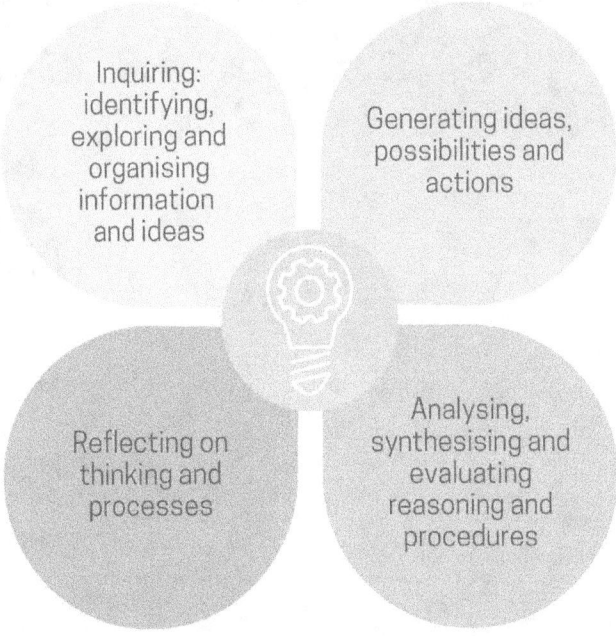

Figure 2: ACARA Critical and Creative Thinking learning elements

Each of the four elements draws upon a range of thinking moves that support students as they think about and engage metacognitively with the content. You will notice that they are not just critical-thinking focused or creative-thinking focused, but rather they draw on both types of thinking to support a particular purpose. As you examine the four elements more closely, you will notice many of the verbs that were highlighted in chapter 1 and begin to see more clearly how the two types of thinking intersect each other.

Element: Inquiring: identifying, exploring and organising information and ideas

This element draws on a range of critical and creative thinking skills, including the ability to pose questions, identify and clarify information, as well as organise and process this information. What is interesting to note is that each 'thinking move', for example, in posing questions, requires students to ask questions in a particular way in order to identify, clarify or compare something. A student's purpose for posing questions and the type of questions they ask is dependent upon a range of factors, such as the age of the learner, content being explored, prior content knowledge as well as the purpose for asking the question.

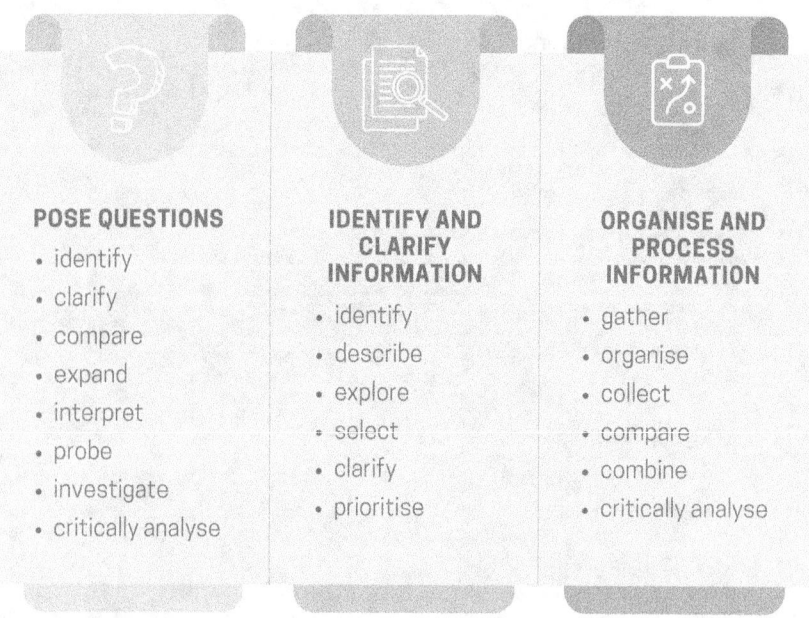

POSE QUESTIONS
- identify
- clarify
- compare
- expand
- interpret
- probe
- investigate
- critically analyse

IDENTIFY AND CLARIFY INFORMATION
- identify
- describe
- explore
- select
- clarify
- prioritise

ORGANISE AND PROCESS INFORMATION
- gather
- organise
- collect
- compare
- combine
- critically analyse

Figure 3: Element: Inquiring: identifying, exploring and organising information and ideas

Reflecting on the element:

- What do you notice about the type of thinking students might be asked to do when undertaking these 'thinking moves'?
- Does critical or creative thinking feature more in this element or is there an equal mix? What makes you think that?
- How might you expect students to develop these skills in your classroom currently? Is it by chance or by design? Why might this be?

Element: Generating ideas, possibilities and actions

This element draws on a range of critical and creative thinking skills, including the ability to imagine possibilities, connect ideas, consider alternatives, seek solutions and put ideas into action. This element requires learners to dig a little deeper into the content, their current understanding and thought processes. You will notice that many of the verbs from the previous element appear again in this element. However, what occurs may indeed be different and more in-depth. For example, the verb 'identify' when looking at information in the previous element requires a different 'level' of thinking to the verb 'identify' when considering alternatives.

While they are the same verb, it is what we ask students to do after the verb 'identify' that determines the depth of thinking required. This element is often regarded as predominantly creative, but it is important to remember that critical and creative thinking often don't occur independently. They are complimentary thought processes that are difficult to separate when arriving at solutions.

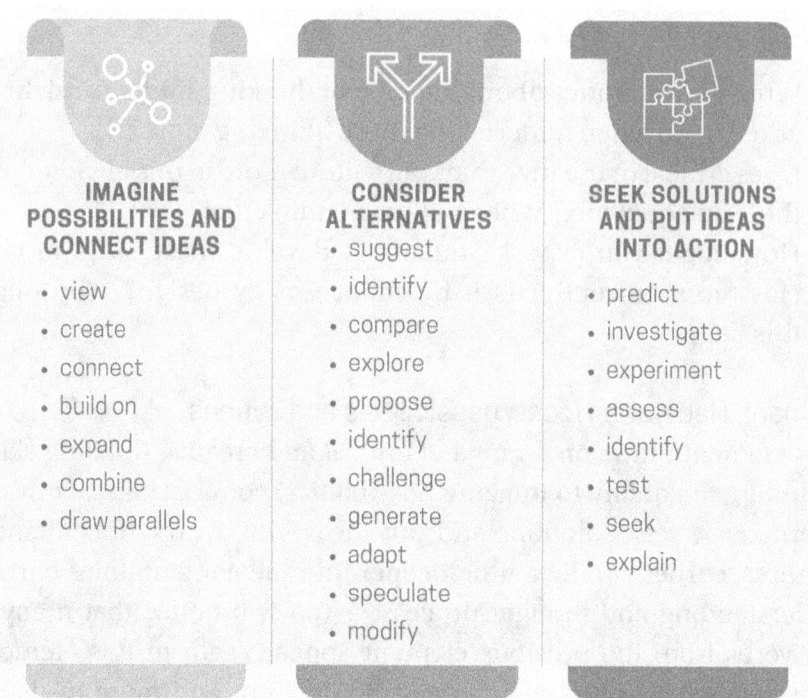

Figure 4: Element: Generating ideas, possibilities and actions

Reflecting on the element:

- What do you notice about the types of thinking students might be asked to do when undertaking these 'thinking moves'?
- How often are students provided with opportunities to generate ideas, possibilities and generate action in their learning?
- How do you currently scaffold this type of thinking?

Element: Analysing, synthesising and evaluating reasoning and procedures

This element draws on a range of critical and creative thinking skills, including the ability to apply logic and reasoning, draw conclusions and design a course of action, alongside evaluate procedures and outcomes. This element adds a layer of complexity to the critical and creative thinking process and as such pushes students towards high-order thinking. This is often the element that students require the most support and scaffolding in order to understand the metacognitive processes required to analyse, synthesise and evaluate using reasoning. The skills of argumentation, drawn from philosophy, can be used to both contextualise and provide structure for the analysis and evaluation of critical and creative thinking (Ellerton, 2017).

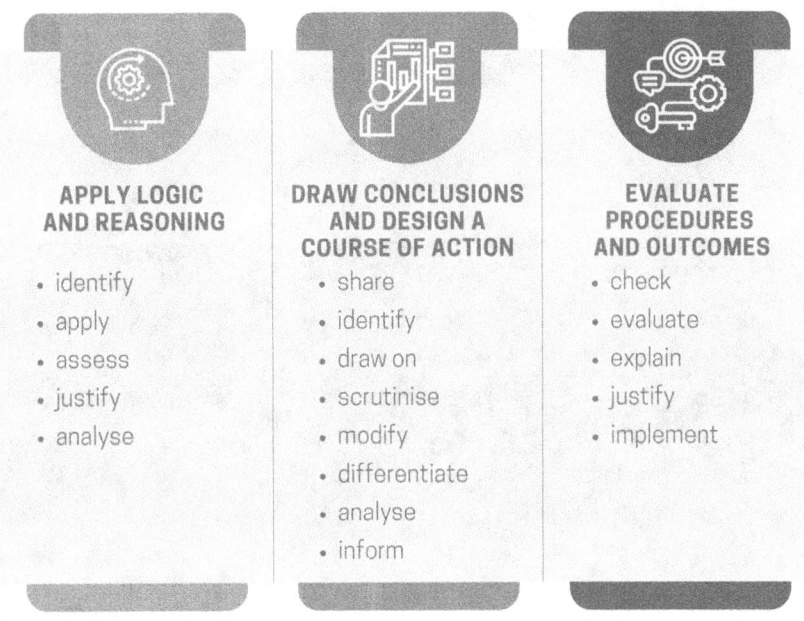

Figure 5: Element: Analysing, synthesising and evaluating reasoning and procedures

Reflecting on the element:

- What do you notice about the types of thinking students might be asked to do when undertaking these 'thinking moves'?
- How often are students provided with opportunities to analyse, synthesise and evaluate using reasoning in their learning?
- How do you currently scaffold this type of thinking?

Element: Reflecting on thinking and processes

This element draws on a range of critical and creative thinking skills, including the ability to think metacognitively, reflect on processes and transfer knowledge to new contexts. This is often the element that gets left behind. Classrooms are extremely busy places and opportunities to reflect on learning, on our thinking and to identify growth in those spaces often falls by the wayside. It is essential that we scaffold and support students in this reflective space in order to support their ability to become independent self-regulated learners, capable of regulating and articulating their thinking at a high level.

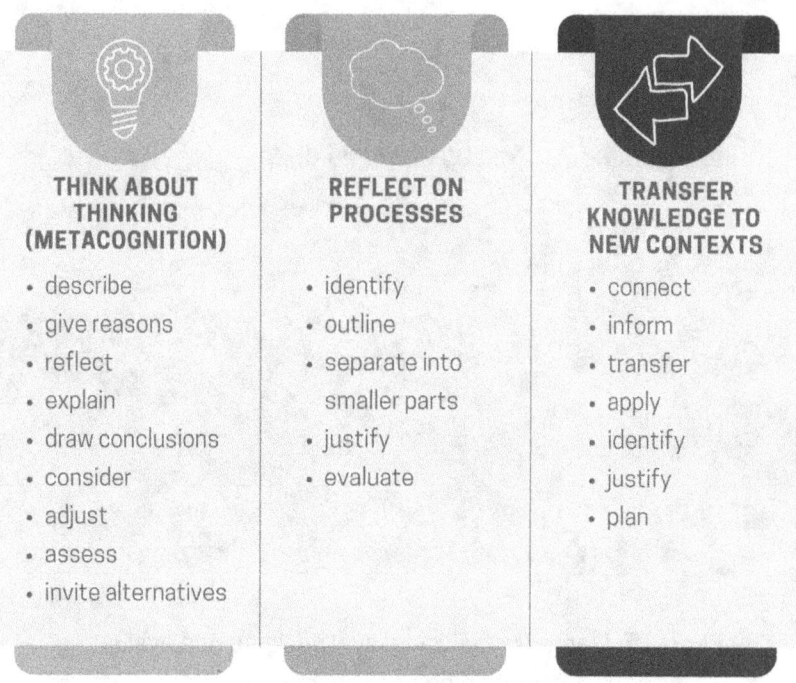

Figure 6: Element: Reflecting on thinking and processes

Reflecting on the element:

- What do you notice about the types of thinking students might be asked to do when undertaking these 'thinking moves'?
- Reflect on the verbs 'justify' and 'give reasons' in this element.
    - How might they be different?
    - What are they asking students to do?
- How might you support students to use the element of reflecting on thinking in your classroom?

Under curriculum reform recommendations, the NSW Department of Education, in partnership with the NSW Education Standards Authority (NESA), seeks to "*make explicit the skills of critical and creative thinking*" and "*sequence content so that deep knowledge and understanding in a subject unfolds*" (Drabsch, 2019; NSW Education Standards Authority, 2020).

McGuinness (1999) argues that curriculum and curriculum reform alone are not enough to raise student learning and achievement outcomes. Attention must be directed to not only what is to be learned (content), but on how children learn (metacognition) and how teachers intervene to achieve this (systems, structures and routines). She highlights that the development of a student's thinking requires 'interventions' to be made at the point of cognitive processing. In order to achieve this, educators need to be explicit in educating directly for critical and creative thinking.

Activity: Critical and Creative Thinking learning continuum

Examine the ACARA Critical and Creative Learning continuum (figure 7) and identify the column that highlights the typical level of thinking for the students in your classroom.

- Choose a range of students from your classroom (up to five) and plot where you think your students' level of thinking is currently.
    - What do you notice about the judgements you made?
    - What evidence of learning did you use to make these judgements?
    - How does your plotting compare to your grade partner or stage team?
    - What evidence of learning might you need to make further judgements about the thinking processes of these students?
- Examine your relevant state's or territory's curriculum documents.
    - Locate an outcome that shows critical and creative thinking as an embedded skill.
    - Identify the type of thinking it is asking students to do.
    - Explain how you might support students to develop their thinking in this content area.
    - How might they transfer this skill to another area of the curriculum?

Critical and Creative Thinking learning continuum

Sub-element	Level 1 Typically, by the end of Foundation Year, students:	Level 2 Typically, by the end of Year 2, students:	Level 3 Typically, by the end of Year 4, students:	Level 4 Typically, by the end of Year 6, students:	Level 5 Typically, by the end of Year 8, students:	Level 6 Typically, by the end of Year 10, students:
Inquiring – identifying, exploring and organising information and ideas element						
Pose questions	pose factual and exploratory questions based on personal interests and experiences	pose questions to identify and clarify issues, and compare information in their world	pose questions to expand their knowledge about the world	pose questions to clarify and interpret information and probe for causes and consequences	pose questions to probe assumptions and investigate complex issues	pose questions to critically analyse complex issues and abstract ideas
Identify and clarify information and ideas	identify and describe familiar information and ideas during a discussion or investigation	identify and explore information and ideas from source materials	identify main ideas and select and clarify information from a range of sources	identify and clarify relevant information and prioritise ideas	clarify information and ideas from texts or images when exploring challenging issues	clarify complex information and ideas drawn from a range of sources
Organise and process information	gather similar information or depictions from given sources	organise information based on similar or relevant ideas from several sources	collect, compare and categorise facts and opinions found in a widening range of sources	analyse, condense and combine relevant information from multiple sources	critically analyse information and evidence according to criteria such as validity and relevance	critically analyse independently sourced information to determine bias and reliability
Generating ideas, possibilities and actions element						
Imagine possibilities and connect ideas	use imagination to view or create things in new ways and connect two things that seem different	build on what they know to create ideas and possibilities in ways that are new to them	expand on known ideas to create new and imaginative combinations	combine ideas in a variety of ways and from a range of sources to create new possibilities	draw parallels between known and new ideas to create new ways of achieving goals	create and connect complex ideas using imagery, analogies and symbolism
Consider alternatives	suggest alternative and creative ways to approach a given situation or task	identify and compare creative ideas to think broadly about a given situation or problem	explore situations using creative thinking strategies to propose a range of alternatives	identify situations where current approaches do not work, challenge existing ideas and generate alternative solutions	generate alternatives and innovative solutions, and adapt ideas, including when information is limited or conflicting	speculate on creative options to modify ideas when circumstances change
Seek solutions and put ideas into action	predict what might happen in a given situation and when putting ideas into action	investigate options and predict possible outcomes when putting ideas into action	experiment with a range of options when seeking solutions and putting ideas into action	assess and test options to identify the most effective solution and to put ideas into action	predict possibilities, and identify and test consequences when seeking solutions and putting ideas into action	assess risks and explain contingencies, taking account of a range of perspectives, when seeking solutions and putting complex ideas into action

Critical and Creative Thinking learning continuum

Sub-element	Level 1 Typically, by the end of Foundation Year, students:	Level 2 Typically, by the end of Year 2, students:	Level 3 Typically, by the end of Year 4, students:	Level 4 Typically, by the end of Year 6, students:	Level 5 Typically, by the end of Year 8, students:	Level 6 Typically, by the end of Year 10, students:
Reflecting on thinking and processes element						
Think about thinking (metacognition)	describe what they are thinking and give reasons why	describe the thinking strategies used in given situations and tasks	reflect on, explain and check the processes used to come to conclusions	reflect on assumptions made, consider reasonable criticism and adjust their thinking if necessary	assess assumptions in their thinking and invite alternative opinions	give reasons to support their thinking, and address opposing viewpoints and possible weaknesses in their own positions
Reflect on processes	identify the main elements of the steps in a thinking process	outline the details and sequence in a whole task and separate it into workable parts	identify pertinent information in an investigation and separate into smaller parts or ideas	identify and justify the thinking behind choices they have made	evaluate and justify the reasons behind choosing a particular problem-solving strategy	balance rational and irrational components of a complex or ambiguous problem to evaluate evidence
Transfer knowledge into new contexts	connect information from one setting to another	use information from a previous experience to inform a new idea	transfer and apply information in one setting to enrich another	apply knowledge gained from one context to another unrelated context and identify new meaning	justify reasons for decisions when transferring information to similar and different contexts	identify, plan and justify transference of knowledge to new contexts
Analysing, synthesising and evaluating reasoning and procedures element						
Apply logic and reasoning	identify the thinking used to solve problems in given situations	identify reasoning used in choices or actions in specific situations	identify and apply appropriate reasoning and thinking strategies for particular outcomes	assess whether there is adequate reasoning and evidence to justify a claim, conclusion or outcome	identify gaps in reasoning and missing elements in information	analyse reasoning used in finding and applying solutions, and in choice of resources
Draw conclusions and design a course of action	share their thinking about possible courses of action	scrutinise ideas or concepts, test conclusions and modify actions when designing a course of action	draw on prior knowledge and use evidence when choosing a course of action or drawing a conclusion	scrutinise ideas or concepts, test conclusions and modify actions when designing a course of action	differentiate the components of a designed course of action and tolerate ambiguities when drawing conclusions	use logical and abstract thinking to analyse and synthesise complex information to inform a course of action
Evaluate procedures and outcomes	check whether they are satisfied with the outcome of tasks or actions	evaluate whether they have accomplished what they set out to achieve	explain and justify ideas and outcomes	evaluate the effectiveness of ideas, products, performances, methods and courses of action against given criteria	explain intentions and justify ideas, methods and courses of action, and account for expected and unexpected outcomes against criteria they have identified	evaluate the effectiveness of ideas, products and performances and implement courses of action to achieve desired outcomes against criteria they have identified

Figure 7: ACARA Critical and Creative Thinking learning continuum

Chapter reflection questions

After reading chapter 2, take a moment to reflect on your learning and understanding.

1. What element of critical and creative thinking is most prevalent in your classroom?
2. What element of critical and creative thinking is least prevalent in your classroom?
3. Why might this be?
4. Describe an experience where you have fostered critical and creative thinking in the past six to 12 months with your students.

PART TWO

PEDAGOGY AND PLANNING FOR THINKING

CHAPTER 3

Explicit teaching, visible learning and the gradual release of responsibility

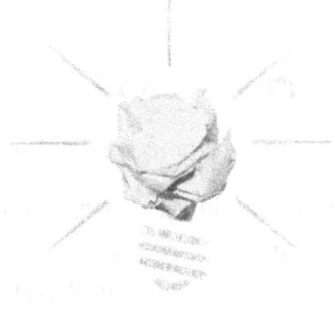

"Learning is a consequence of thinking, not something extra we tack on for good measure but something in which we must actively engage to promote our own and others' learning"

Ron Ritchhart, Creating Cultures of Thinking (2015)

Every educator knows there are a variety of pedagogical practices and strategies that they employ in classrooms on a regular basis. What is crucial for educators to know and understand is how the practices they currently utilise can be leveraged to explicitly and systematically support the development of critical and creative thinking in the classroom. The practices outlined in this and the preceding chapter are not new and have been part of the fabric of classrooms for decades. What is most important to remember is that with any approach we employ, teaching must lead to learning, through the development of knowledge, skills and confidence that students need to think critically and creatively, learn deeply and experience opportunities to apply this across disciplines in a systematic and structured way.

This chapter explores the key role that explicit teaching, visible learning and the gradual release of responsibility play in fostering the thinking skills of students in the classroom, and outlines how teachers can leverage these in their practice as they begin to examine learning through the lens of strong content knowledge, and critical and creative thinking.

Chapter learning intentions

By the end of this chapter, educators will be able to:

- Explain the pedagogical practices that support critical and creative thinking
- Identify strategies that can be employed in their teaching practice
- Understand the role of explicit instruction in scaffolding thinking moves for students

Leveraging explicit instruction

It may sound counterproductive, but being explicit in our modelling and instruction, alongside scaffolding the thought process, is key to building a culture of critical and creative thinkers and learners in the classroom. As educators, we all walk through the school gates with the same goal:

> *"To help students make the maximum possible academic gains in a positive, respectful environment that promotes their success and nurtures their desire to learn."*
>
> *(Archer & Hughes, 2011)*

Through employing an explicit teaching approach to instruction, educators remove the ambiguity around instructional design and delivery procedures. Explicit teaching is a structured, systematic and effective methodology for teaching (Archer & Hughes, 2011). It is characterised by a series of supports or scaffolds that are designed to guide students through the learning process. Providing clarity about the purpose and rationale for learning, alongside modelling of the instructional target and identifying markers of success, are key features of this pedagogical approach. Ongoing feedback about the development of student thinking related to key content knowledge as well as reflection on growth in understanding through structured processes is another key element of an explicit instruction approach.

According to the Centre for Education Statistics and Evaluation (CESE), the research highlights that students who experience explicit instruction demonstrate increased academic achievement in comparison to those who do not. The evidence suggests that it has wide-ranging benefits for all students, regardless of their age or ability level, when learning new or complex skills (Centre for Education Statistics and Evaluation, 2020). This is due to the structured and systematic way in which educators utilise this pedagogical approach to 'chunk' learning in order to reduce the cognitive load for students when learning new things and linking this learning to their prior knowledge.

Underpinning explicit instruction are 10 core principles that are grounded in research around how the brain learns new information and research on high-performing teachers and their classroom practices (Rosenshine, 2010). It is through these 10 core principles that we will examine how educators can leverage explicit instruction in the classroom to support the development of critical and creative thinking skills. The 10 core principles are:

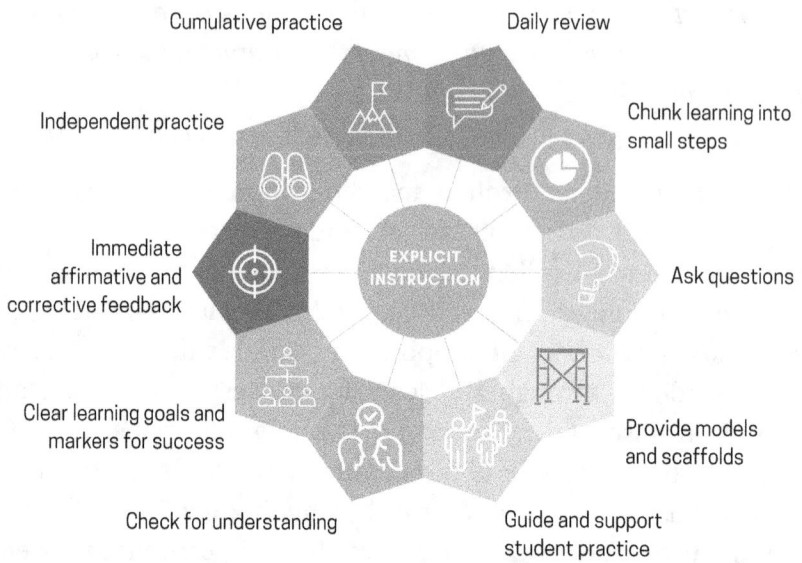

Figure 8: Principles of explicit instruction

1. Daily review

   An important component of instruction that helps students to strengthen the connections they have made to concepts and skills previously learnt and might be required to draw upon during the learning cycle that day. Utilising this element allows teachers to provide additional practice on facts and skills that were needed for recall to become automatic (Sherrington, 2019).

   In the classroom

   Daily review takes as little as five to eight minutes each day to practise skills or review concepts. In a classroom that actively fosters and values critical and creative thinking, this might be reviewing some thinking about a concept or topic previously taught, such as examining and discussing thoughts and ideas documented previously in a Geography unit.

2. Chunk learning into small steps

   In order to reduce the cognitive load for learners, educators should break down learning into manageable 'chunks' and support students as they engage with the material.

In the classroom
The notion of 'chunking' learning into small steps supports students as they learn to think more critically and creatively about the content they are engaging with. When teachers break down the thought process required to know and understand a concept or skill to the point of mastery, only then can students confidently build upon and deepen their level of understanding. An example of this might be the use of a thinking routine to break down the thought process into parts.

3. Ask questions
   Questions helps students to practise new information and connect new material to their prior learning (Rosenshine, 2010).

   In the classroom
   The art of questioning serves two purposes in the thinking classroom. First, it allows for students to make connections between new concepts and their prior learning. Second, it provides teachers with a snapshot of which students have a good handle on the concept and if there is a need for additional instruction (Sherrington, 2019). In the thinking classroom, questioning sits at the heart of classroom thinking and discussion, such as using questioning prompts to help students unpack their thoughts and opinions.

4. Provide models and scaffolds
   Students require cognitive support to help them learn to solve problems. The use of scaffolds helps to provide those supports to learners as they break down the learning process into parts or 'chunks'.

   In the classroom
   In the critical and creative thinking classroom, educators can draw upon supports such as modelling, think alouds, worked examples and learning scaffolds to reduce the cognitive load on students' working memory. For example, using the thinking routine See Think Wonder might help students to notice elements, think about the importance of those elements to the whole and ask questions to drive further learning.

5. Guide and support student practice
   Providing students with the opportunity to engage with guided learning increases a student's ability to work independently without difficulty on a concept or skill.

   In the classroom
   Guided learning in the classroom is an important component of supporting student thinking. If we want students to interact with a concept or think about a piece of information in a particular way, then we need to provide opportunities to guide them through this process in a 'chunked' and scaffolded way.

6. Check for understanding
   Checking for understanding occurs on a regular basis and allows educators to determine if students are grasping the concepts being explored and determine if any misconceptions are developing (Rosenshine, 2010).

   In the classroom
   One way that educators can effectively check for understanding is to ask students questions. Questions such as *What makes you say that?* asks students to explain their thinking about the information they are learning.

7. Clear learning goals and markers for success
   Providing students with a clear statement about what is to be learnt during the lesson, why it is important and what it will look like when we have successfully achieved our learning goals is essential to providing clarity to students about the learning journey.

   In the classroom
   It is important that teachers provide clear statements about what is being learnt. Using sentence stems, such as *We are learning to...* or posing learning intentions as a question, such as *How do animals adapt to a changing climate?* supports the transference of learning. Indicating markers of success also supports students to know and understand how they can measure success along the way and how they will be assessed on their learning. This concept is unpacked further in the 'Making learning visible' section of this chapter.

8. **Immediate affirmative and corrective feedback**
   Follow up on student responses as quickly as you can. Immediate feedback to students about the accuracy of their responses helps ensure high rates of success and reduces the likelihood of practising errors (Archer & Hughes, 2011).

   In the classroom
   The goal of feedback is to close the gap between a student's current understanding and the desired understanding in order to improve their growth and achievement. In a classroom that makes thinking visible and valued, providing students with affirmative and corrective feedback allows them to understand ways to build on their thought processes, draw connections and build a deeper understanding of key curriculum concepts.

9. **Independent practice**
   A key feature of all classrooms is the opportunity for students to apply their learning and current understanding to an independent learning task. It is a process that supports students as they learn to become fluent with skills, facts, concepts and the ability to discriminate between new learning and prior learning (Rosenshine, 2010).

   In the classroom
   Independent practice is a prime opportunity for students to practise the skills they learnt and refined during guided learning opportunities. Drawing on *Assessment As Learning* frameworks during this phase is a powerful opportunity for students to teach or explain concepts to one another, such as peer feedback.

10. **Cumulative practice**
    Learning is most powerful when it can be refined, built upon and mastered over time. Sherrington (2019) highlights that students need to be involved in extensive practice in order to develop well-connected and automatic knowledge.

    In the classroom
    Providing students with multiple opportunities to practise a skill or learn about and apply concepts over time is hugely beneficial to

retention, fluency and automaticity. Combined with new learning, this allows students to make greater connections and build a broader depth of understanding (Archer & Hughes, 2011).

Utilising explicit instruction when helping students to build their cognitive and metacognitive processes allows both teachers and students to make thinking visible and valued. It is through this pedagogical practice that teachers can leverage other practices such as thinking routines to carefully scaffold the thought process of students through the vehicle of curriculum content.

Embedding the gradual release of responsibility framework

The gradual release of responsibility model of instruction suggests that cognitive work should shift slowly and intentionally from teacher modelling to joint responsibility between teachers and students, to independent practice and application by the learner (Frey & Fisher, 2013). It is a model or framework that is based on the belief that teachers can be intentional about the increase in student ownership of their learning over time. The use of the gradual release of responsibility framework helps educators to leverage explicit instruction in the classroom through establishing the purpose for learning, modelling cognitive processes, scaffolding the learning process, guiding learning, checking understanding and providing feedback, as well as being intentional about opportunities for independent practice.

The framework is most commonly comprised of three core practices:

1. I DO – focused instruction
2. WE DO – guided instruction
3. YOU DO – independent learning

Douglas Fisher and Nancy Frey in their book, *Better Learning Through Structured Teaching: A Framework for the Gradual Release of Responsibility*, suggest that a fourth and crucial component should be considered for this framework – that being the interactions that come from working collaboratively with peers. They therefore express a four-tiered model for the gradual release of responsibility (2021). Figure 9 moulds these two versions of the framework together, incorporating 'you do it together' and 'you do it alone' together as two components of the You Do phase – independent and collaborative learning.

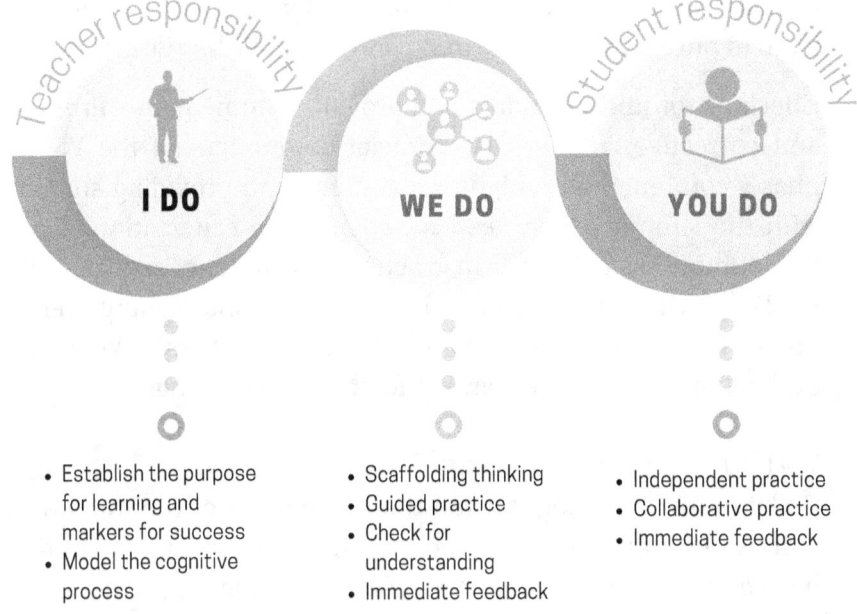

Figure 9: The gradual release of responsibility framework

1. I DO – focused instruction

   In this phase of the framework the focus is on establishing a purpose for the lesson and strongly links with the visible learning practices of learning intentions and success criteria. Teacher modelling and think alouds are also key features of this phase.

   It is in this phase of the gradual release of responsibility model that educators can be intentional about showing students what breaking down the thinking process into manageable 'chunks' looks and sounds like. When educators do this, students are able to see and hear effective thinking in action, watch as the teacher applies different cognitive processes and gain a deeper understanding of what they will need to do during the We Do and You Do phases of the framework. Modelling the use of scaffolds and thinking routines is also beneficial in this phase.

2. WE DO – guided instruction

   In this phase of the framework, teachers scaffold the thinking and understanding of students. Instructional scaffolds are an essential element of this phase and strongly correlate with the use of thinking routines. The use of robust questioning prompts and cues to facilitate and scaffold student thinking when necessary, as students learn to put new knowledge into play (Frey & Fisher, 2013).

   Checking for understanding and providing immediate affirmative and corrective feedback is a crucial component of the We Do phase, combined with high expectations and providing students with the supports they need to reach those expectations forms the foundations of guided instruction. All students engage in the We Do phase, regardless of ability level. This phase should reflect point of need for students, which requires teachers to know and understand their learners and differentiate accordingly.

3. YOU DO – collaborative learning

   Collaborative learning is often the component of the framework that is left out, possibly due to time constraints or student behaviours among other things. However, when implemented as an established instructional routine, it can support students in consolidating their thinking and expanding their understanding. It is when we are asked to talk through our thinking, elaborate, explain and justify to others our ideas that new learning and prior learning are powerfully meshed together. This phase is not the opportunity to introduce new concepts, but is a time for students to apply what they already know in novel situations or engage in a spiral review of previous knowledge (Fisher & Frey, 2021).

4. YOU DO – independent learning

   The ultimate goal of instruction is for students to be able to independently apply thinking, information, ideas, content, skills and strategies to unique situations. It is important that educators provide rich opportunities for students to 'practise' completing independent tasks in a supportive environment, receiving and engaging with feedback in order to learn from those tasks. Fisher and Frey (2021) highlight:

"What is essential for an independent learning task is that it clearly links and relates to the instruction each student received yet also provide the student an opportunity to apply the resulting knowledge in a new way."

Embedding the gradual release of responsibility framework into the classroom is a powerful way for teachers to break down the learning and thinking process into manageable 'chunks', reducing the cognitive load for students. While visually a simple framework, the gradual release model supports teachers to be intentional about their instructional teaching time. It causes them to 'pause' and think about the phases of the learning cycle and how and when to move students through those phases.

It is a framework that helps to support the scaffolding of critical and/or creative thinking skills for our students as we intentionally model, name and notice thinking in the classroom. Modelling is crucial to supporting the cognitive and metacognitive processes of our students. If we don't know what it is like to be an effective thinker and to intentionally think in critical and creative ways, then how might we be able to apply these skills effectively?

The act of modelling our thinking and naming what we are doing through think alouds allows our students to see and hear what effective thinkers do, giving them a clear model for what it is you, as the educator, are looking for from them. This supports 'focusing the lesson' as the teacher works to demystify the type(s) of thinking being asked of the students, for example, to notice, wonder or examine. Equally, scaffolding provides a critical 'safety net' for students as they learn to experiment, notice and name the different types of thinking they are doing.

Making learning visible

"Know thy impact."
(Professor John Hattie, Visible Learning for Teachers, *2012)*

Using visible learning pedagogical approaches is another way we can leverage critical and creative thinking in any classroom. Visible learning comes from the research and works of Professor John Hattie and is a big part of evidence-based best practice in the classroom. Visible learning stems from 15 years of research from Professor Hattie, which is based on millions of students and represented the largest meta-analysis and synthesis of what improves student learning outcomes. It means an enhanced role for teachers as they become more reflective and evaluative of their own pedagogy. Visible teaching and learning occur when thinking and learning processes are visible, meaningful, shareable and amplified (Vigors, 2018).

As we have previously discussed in this chapter, establishing the purpose for learning and markers for success are crucial components to the development of students' critical and creative thinking. Students need to know what they are learning, the type of thinking required to undertake that learning and what success will look like along the way. Providing clarity to learners about the intent for learning and the success measures demystifies the learning process and removes the element of 'guess what's in the teacher's head'.

Learning intentions

Learners tend to learn more effectively when they are clear about the purpose of learning. Knowing where you are headed does not mean that the tasks need to have every single detail mapped out for you, but it does require a clarity of the purpose of learning. The intentions we have for students' learning should be clear. They should never be a secret or guess what's in the teacher's head. Consistently utilising learning intentions provides a rich opportunity for teachers to frame the *why* behind the learning.

Why is this learning important to us?

Why does this learning matter?

Learning intentions help us to set students up for success as we support the development of their metacognitive thinking skills. Ensuring that students understand and can recognise the type of metacognitive thinking required to undertake a learning task is equally as important.

As educators, we need to explain the type of thinking students are required to use during a learning task, as well as highlight a sound example of what this thinking looks like in order to be successful. This also means students need explicit guidance and practice in knowing how to think in different ways and be able to apply this to a variety of everyday situations (Vigors, 2018).

Success criteria

Success criteria are the measures used to determine whether, and how well, learners have met the learning intentions (Australian Institute for Teaching and School Leadership, 2017). It provides a clear scaffold and focus for learners while engaging with the learning. It is important to remember that the success criteria we provide or co-construct with students directly links back to the learning intentions.

When students have success criteria at hand, they are more informed about how they will be assessed. Consequently, they are better able to assess their own and others' work to identify successes and areas for improvement.

Success criteria are most effective when they:

- Link to the learning intention
- Are specific to a learning experience or task
- Are discussed, co-constructed and agreed with learners prior to undertaking the learning experience
- Use child-friendly language
- Are visible and referred to during the learning experience
- Provide a clear scaffold and focus for learners while engaging with the learning
- Are used as the basis for feedback between learner and teacher, and during peer and self-assessment
- Are tangible and measurable

It is essential that success criteria are not just for students but for teachers, too. The development of success criteria provides a rich opportunity for teachers to be specific and intentional about the feedback being provided to our students – focusing on the process of learning rather than just a 'well done response'. Providing immediate affirmative and corrective feedback linked to the success criteria helps teachers to remain focused on the intention for learning, the thinking skills required and the process of learning we are wanting students to demonstrate. Approaching feedback in this way means our feedback is focused, timely and constructive, increasing the likelihood that students will be able to act upon the feedback to improve learning.

It is in using visible learning practices like learning intentions and success criteria that we can support students in understanding the types of thinking required of them during the lesson in order to be successful. The more students are able to notice and name the types of thinking they are doing, the better they will get at being able to recognise opportunities when a particular type or types of thinking will be required to undertake a certain task.

Why verbs matter

Verbs by their very definition are words used to show an action (list), an occurrence (develop) or a state of being (exist). It is through the use of verbs in a learning intention and success criteria that educators are able to highlight the type of thinking required by the students.

Activity: What's the verb got to do with it?

Reflect on a learning intention and accompanying success criteria you have planned (or maybe already taught) over the past two weeks.

- What verbs were used?
- What type(s) of thinking were you asking your students to do?
- How did you provide clarity to your students about what this type of thinking looks and sounds like?
- If no clarity was provided, reflect on why not.
- What might you change or adapt next time you plan learning intentions and success criteria?

Chapter reflection questions

After reading chapter 3, take a moment to reflect on your learning and understanding.

1. How do you currently utilise explicit instruction in your practice?
2. How might you change or adapt what you currently do to be explicit, systematic and intentional about teaching critical and creative thinking skills?
3. How do you or might you utilise the gradual release of responsibility to support and scaffold the thinking processes of your students?
4. What role does the visible learning practice of learning intentions and success criteria play in your current practice?
5. How might you utilise this practice as a springboard to noticing and naming the types of thinking a lesson sequence is asking of students in order to be successful learners?
6. What do the verbs you use and the types of tasks you assign say about the types of thinking you value?
7. Do you use and assign mostly lower-order thinking tasks or a mix of lower-order building to higher-order?

CHAPTER 4

Thinking routines and the art of questioning

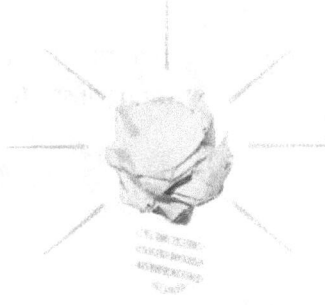

"If we are trying to understand something, we have to notice its parts and features, being able to describe it fully and in detail"

Ron Ritchhart and colleagues, Making Thinking Visible (2011)

Learning is a complex and evolving process that requires the interplay of effective instruction, content, thought processes, knowledge and skills. At the intersection of these are key scaffolds and robust questions educators ask to support and enhance student learning. For learning to truly be a consequence of thinking, educators need to know and understand how to utilise different types of critical and creative thinking moves across different learning situations and tasks.

This chapter explores the key role thinking routines, and questioning play in scaffolding and deepening the thinking skills of students in the classroom. It outlines how teachers can leverage these in their practice as they begin to examine learning through the lens of critical and creative thinking.

Chapter learning intentions

By the end of this chapter, educators will be able to:

- Explain the role of thinking routines in supporting metacognition
- Understand the phases of development and their implications on the development of student thinking in the classroom
- Identify the role of questioning in the classroom

Thinking routines

Thinking routines have been cultivated and researched by Ron Ritchhart, Mark Church and the team at Harvard's Project Zero for many years and are the culmination of working with many teachers around the world to understand the role of thinking routines on students' ability to think – and think well. Every classroom is dominated by a range of routines. There are instructional routines, behavioural routines, organisational routines and communication routines to name but a few. Through the research, Ritchhart discovered that educators who successfully promoted student thinking did so using and adapting specific routines to support student thinking (2011).

When we demystify the thinking and learning process, we provide models for students of what it means to engage with ideas, to think and to learn. One way that we can provide a framework and scaffold for fostering metacognitive practices is through the use of thinking routines. Thinking routines are easy-to-use scaffolds that can be repeatedly used in the classroom across a variety of content and grade levels. They provide a structure to support students in the process of thinking about thinking and breaking down their thought processes in different ways. Routines take on more power when they are used to support students' ongoing learning.

Each routine targets a different kind of thinking, and by bringing their own content, teachers integrate the routines into the fabric of their classrooms. Each thinking routine provides a way to embed formative assessment into the teaching and learning process. Formative assessment lives in our listening, observing, examining, analysing and reflecting on the process of learning and using the data to inform our teaching and students' learning. Routines also help to direct student thinking and provide structure to classroom discussion. There is an abundance of thinking routines that can be used and adapted for specific purposes and types of thinking.

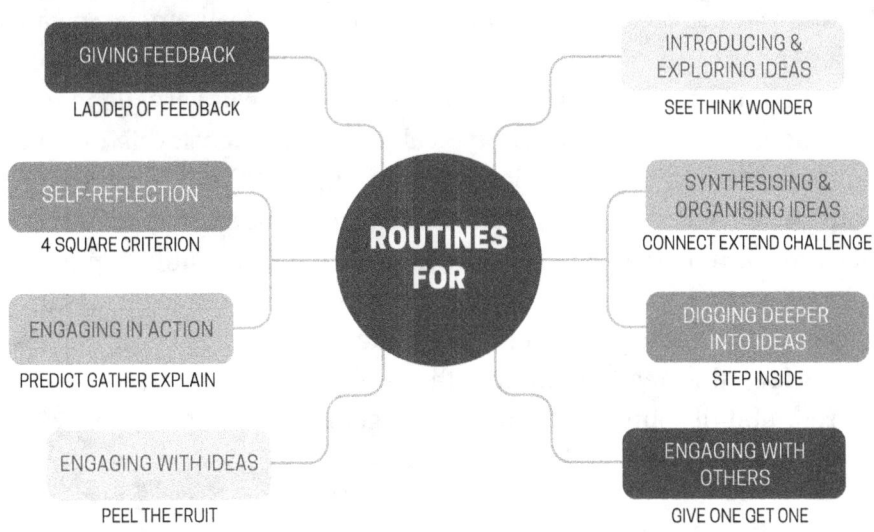

Figure 10: Types of thinking routines (Ritchhart et al 2011)

As figure 10 highlights, there is a large range of thinking routines that are categorised according to purpose and function. Each routine combines a unique set of thinking 'moves' in order to understand a concept or skill in a specific and structured way. In part four of this book, we take a closer look at some of these thinking routines and how we can apply them to specific curriculum areas. These are a collection of the most widely used routines in my classroom and provide a snapshot of what they look like in action with my students.

? How does explicit instruction and the gradual release of responsibility fit with the use of thinking routines?

Utilising thinking routines in conjunction with explicit instruction and the gradual release of responsibility is akin to a builder using scaffolding when constructing a building. A large amount of scaffolding is used as construction work begins, but the more work that is undertaken on the building, the less reliant on the scaffolding the workers become. The scaffolding is removed in clear stages until the building stands on its own.

Through deliberate, careful and temporary scaffolding, students can learn new basic skills as well as more complex skills, maintain a high level of success as they do so and systematically move towards independent use of the skill. The amount of initial support needed and the rate at which the support is withdrawn will vary, depending on students' needs. Teachers typically provide high levels of initial guidance and then systematically reduce support as students respond with greater accuracy. As guidance is reduced, students are required to perform with increasing independence until they are able to perform the skill on their own. Scaffolding is an effective approach for ensuring success and building confidence for students while they learn, because it provides the needed support that helps bridge the gap between current abilities and the instructional goal (Archer & Hughes, 2011; Rosenshine, 1995).

The use of scaffolding through intentionally embedding thinking routines into the gradual release of responsibility model draws on a number of the principles of explicit instruction highlighted in the previous chapter, including:

- Chunking learning into small steps
- Providing models and scaffolds of what the thinking process looks and sounds like
- Guided practice
- Checking for understanding
- Asking questions

As Archer and Hughes (2011) highlight, scaffolding is an effective approach to building the success and confidence of students throughout the learning process, as it provides the needed support that helps bridge the gap between what a student currently knows, understands and is able to do, and the instructional goal.

Phases of thinking development

When using thinking routines as strategic vehicles in which to scaffold the thinking of our learners, we need to consider, as teachers, where we (both teacher and learner) are at in the phases of development continuum.

Is this the first time you have used this routine?

Or have you been using it regularly for a while now?

Or is it so ingrained your learners use it without realising it?

The answers to these questions will depend on the routine you are using and how often it is used within your educational context. It is therefore conceivable that a learner could be at varying phases at the same time for different routines (Vigors, 2019).

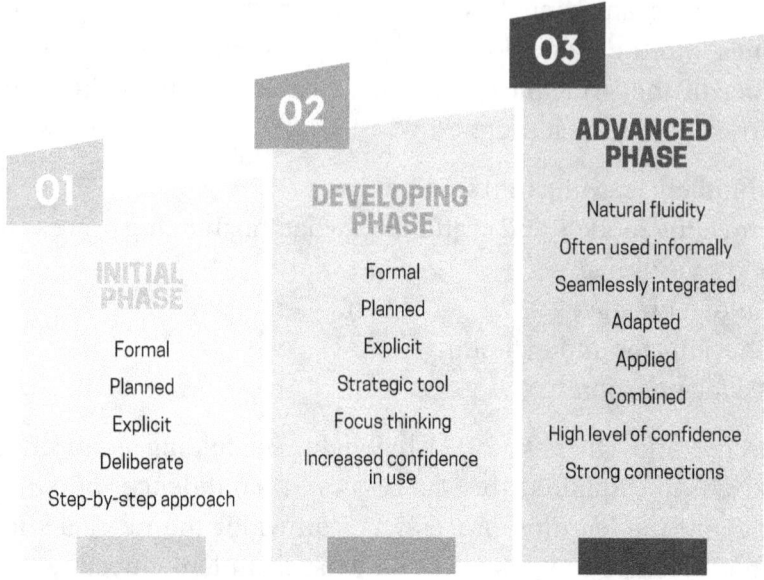

Figure 11: Phases of thinking development

Initial phase

When a routine is introduced for the very first time to students in a classroom, it is formal, deliberate, explicit and planned. The teacher explicitly structures the thinking routine in a step-by-step manner in order to scaffold student thinking at each point. This results in deliberate 'chunking' of the content and metacognitive processes simultaneously to reduce the cognitive load for students.

For example, a teacher introduces the thinking routine See Think Wonder (Ritchhart et al, 2011) to their students during an English lesson involving visual imagery. The teacher is familiar with the stimulus and is deliberate in their use of think alouds and prompting to support students through the phases or steps of this routine. They begin with the 'See' component – *What do you see? What do you observe? What do you notice?* Dependent on the teacher confidence with the routine and the learner understanding of the vocabulary being used, the teacher may ask only *What do you see?* Or all three prompts to ask students to look at the image and provide only facts about what is noticed. This could be undertaken orally or involve a written component.

Teachers would then transition students to the 'Think' phase using the prompt *What do you think is happening?* It is through this prompt that teachers are asking students to draw on their prior knowledge, combined with information gathered through noticing to draw inferences about what is occurring in the image. The final phase is 'Wonder'. It is in this phase that teachers gather student wonderings about the visual prompt using the sentence stem *What do you wonder?* This phase is a powerful part of the routine and supports teachers as they seek to drive learning forwards.

It is important to remember that when introducing any new thinking routine into the classroom that teachers are strategic about its use, engage with it frequently and look for opportunities to experiment with the thinking routine in other areas of the curriculum, thus providing the platform for learners to apply thinking 'moves' across disciplines as well as transition to the next phase of thinking development.

Developing phase

A learner that has transitioned a thinking routine to the developing phase is increasingly used as more of a tool to delve into the curriculum content and understandings. It becomes an overt tool to focus student thinking and direct learning in a way that is planned and explicit. In this phase learners are becoming more and more confident and comfortable with the routine, recognising when the teacher is employing the routine and identifying the steps required to undertake the thinking routine with fidelity. The developing phase sees students as well as teachers being able to utilise a thinking routine to support the development of understanding across a variety of curriculum areas. Branching into this phase supports learners as they begin to see how particular 'thinking moves' might be usefully applied to a range of situations and problems.

For example, the teacher using the See Think Wonder thinking routine with a visual stimulus recognises that there might be benefits to utilising the same routine when examining population growth data over time in the Geography or Mathematics classroom. The teacher in this instance experiments with the routine in a different curriculum area or component of a single curriculum area to look at how the 'thinking moves' transfer to different situations depending on the content through which the thinking routine drives the learning. The transition to the developing phase allows both the teacher and students to see how metacognitive processes are not subject specific, rather, they support the development of understanding across a broad range of subject matter.

Looking back at the example of examining population growth in Geography or Mathematics, the teacher may begin by displaying the data to be examined and ask students *What do you see, observe or notice?* This part of the routine asks students to focus purely on the facts and what the data is showing them. For example, the title, the x and y axis labels, the height of the columns in a column graph or the rise and fall of the line in a line graph. The teacher then draws the attention of students to a particular component of the data using the prompt *What do you think?* This prompt asks students to make inferences about why something is represented in this way and what that might tell us, before finally diving into wonderings about the data using the prompt *What do you wonder?* This final prompt provides a rich platform from which to springboard into future learning opportunities as students seek to make sense of and develop subject-specific content knowledge.

Advanced phase

When a learner is comfortable and confident with using and applying a routine to a range of situations without the need for explicit scaffolding, then they have transitioned the use of the thinking routine to the advanced phase of thinking development. Learners operating at this level conduct the routine with a natural fluidity from one part to the next – it is not rigid or conducted in a step-by-step approach as is the case in the initial phase.

A learner working at the advanced level is able to apply the thinking routine seamlessly; combining, adapting and integrating it across curriculum content, knowledge and skills in order to support their development of thinking and depth of understanding. In this phase, learners begin to apply the thinking routine to learning experiences without being formally used by the teacher to help them unpack their thinking processes and deepen their understanding. It is in this phase that learners are able to recognise the value of a 'thinking move' or routine in helping them to make sense of concepts.

The art of questioning

Questioning is inextricably linked to learning and sits at the heart of the classroom. It is the vessel through which we can help to make our own and others' thinking visible. The power of a single question has the ability to show you how a student thinks, the depth of their thought processes and their ability to connect their background knowledge and prior learning to new concepts. It becomes a powerful observation tool when applied effectively in the classroom setting. Questioning underpins the use of thinking routines and is the basis from which they support metacognitive processes and the ability to 'chunk' learning into manageable components.

Warren Berger and Elise Foster, in their book *Beautiful Questions in the Classroom* (2020), highlight five key reasons why questioning is central to future success in our society:

1. **Innovation** – questioning is often the starting point of innovation
2. **Serial mastery** – questioning helps us keep adding new skills and adapting to change
3. **Critical thinking** – questioning helps us sort through the abundance of information
4. **Creativity** – questioning sparks new ideas
5. **Lifelong learning** – questioning is a primary tool for continually expanding knowledge

Research tells us that questioning has a positive impact on student learning and is the signature of outstanding pedagogical practice. It is through the art of questioning that learners can discover and uncover new meaning, providing a valuable bridge from what is known to a connection with what is new. In the 21st century, access to information is abundant and students need to be able to discern what is relevant and reliable from what is not. They require the skills to not only be able to answer thought-provoking questions from their teachers, but to feel comfortable enough to ask questions in the classroom.

Fostering an environment where students feel safe to ask questions is an important part of shaping a classroom of curious learners. This space should be one that allows students to see and hear wonderings, curiosities and uncertainties from both the teacher and their peers, but to also see and hear our willingness to find out things when we don't know (Murdoch, 2015). As we have discussed earlier, modelling our thinking and using think alouds are powerful tools in inviting students into the space of questioning.

Reflection: Take a moment to reflect on your classroom today, yesterday or last week.

- *How many questions did you ask your students that promoted learning and metacognitive processes?*
- *How many questions did your students ask you that supported their learning or thought processes?*

Reflecting on the types of questions teachers and students pose helps us to think about and understand the 'why' behind the questions being asked. Commonly, there are two types of questions people ask: open and closed. Kath Murdoch highlights that questioning does not happen in a vacuum. Effective questioning is closely linked to aspects such as a person's comfort levels, willingness to share their thinking, understanding of key vocabulary and their familiarity with the content (2015).

Developing a classroom that thrives on questions

In my classroom, if students aren't asking rich and thought-provoking questions, then I've missed the mark. As educators, we want classrooms that are full of questions from not only the teacher, but from the students as well. When students set about answering a question, they begin to construct ideas, apply knowledge, absorb new information and demonstrate understanding. Open, rich, engaging questions are a consistent feature of a classroom that thrives on questioning. In order to bring this rich tapestry to life, there are a number of key things educators can do to leverage a culture of questioning, including modelling, fostering curiosity and scaffolding.

Modelling and fostering curiosity

Provoking and modelling a curious disposition across the day is critical. If we want to see a culture of questioning develop, then we as educators need to be the ones leading the way and showing learners what this looks, sounds and feels like. Just like we do when we use learning intentions and success criteria to provide clarity to learners about the learning journey, modelling ourselves as questioners is crucial to supporting students' understanding of what a curious, questioning learner demonstrates.

Valued, visible and actively promoted

Valuing and working with students' questions and building their questioning skills and knowledge goes a long way to building a culture of questioning in the classroom. Take the time to truly listen to the questions your learners are asking. Show them that their questions and thoughts matter and are valuable to our learning. This can be achieved by modelling what we do when we ask rich questions, how we solve these questions and why we reflect on the information we've learned.

Scaffolding

Planning learning experiences around questions through utilising sophisticated and thoughtful questioning and dialogue techniques in the classroom also supports a culture of questioning. The use of thinking routines is a powerful tool to support this process. Educators need to choose questioning and routines that are fit for purpose and support the development of understanding about the content that is being explored. Scaffolds that support 'thinking moves' through questioning should never be used in isolation without core content to give them purpose, meaning and value.

Research conducted by Hopkins and Craig highlights that questioning plays a large part in our classrooms, being the second most utilised teaching strategy behind teacher talk. However, most of the questions that we ask our students are lower-order or lower-cognitive questions that ask them to recall facts or are procedural. This is indicative of a focus on knowledge acquisition (2015). Utilising higher-order questioning enables students to convert information to knowledge and move from knowledge acquisition to knowledge application. It is important to emphasise, as brain studies show, that motivation to learn is not sustained simply by asking questions. It is sustained by identifying, explaining and using the new knowledge and understanding that results from asking and responding to questions.

Most researchers agree that a combination of lower- and higher-order questions is far superior to the exclusive use of one or the other. As Murdoch highlights, lower-order questions may be needed to scaffold thinking to higher levels, just as having a surface-level understanding is an important base for building depth and breadth of knowledge, and being able to then apply that understanding, which will be explored further in part three (2015).

As teachers who are committed to fostering student curiosity and thinking, it is our job to ensure that we are providing opportunities for students to think about and answer a range of questions, particularly higher-order questions. Students also need to learn how to ask questions, both of themselves as they are learning, and of the ideas they are learning about. The following continuum of thinking skills can be a useful prompt to help teachers and students scaffold a range of different questions throughout the learning process (Vigors, 2019).

← LOWER-ORDER QUESTIONING | HIGHER-ORDER QUESTIONING →

Knowledge	Comprehension	Application	Analysis	Synthesis	Evaluation
Memory is used to **recall** previously learned material such as facts, terms, definitions, basic concepts and answers.	**Constructing meaning** from different types of texts in order to demonstrate understanding of facts and ideas.	To **apply** learning to a **new situation**. Solving problems by applying acquired knowledge, facts, techniques and rules in different ways.	To **examine** information and break it into parts in order to examine details, make connections, infer and support, ideas and arguments.	To **change** or **create** into something new by combining information and ideas in different and more creative ways to propose alternative solutions.	To **justify** thinking and present judgements, recommendations and defend opinions.
Question stems	**Question stems**	**Question stems**	**Question stems**	**Question stems**	**Question stems**
• Can you recall…? • Can you list…? • What does… mean? • Who was…? • Where is…? • How would you describe…? • How did… happen? • What is…? • Where is…? • Why did…? • When did…?	• What is the main idea of…? • What might happen next? • Can you retell… in your own words? • What is meant by…? • What facts or ideas show…? • How would you summarise…?	• How would you use…? • Could this have happened in…? • What would happen if…? • What approach would you use to…? • What would result if…? • What questions would you ask…?	• Why do you think…? • How does… compare to…? • What evidence can you find…? • What is the theme? • What conclusions can we make? • What is… motive? • What ideas justify…?	• What changes would you make to find…? • How would you improve…? • What would happen if…? • Can you predict the outcome of…? • Can you construct a model that can…?	• What is your opinion of…? • Why did… choose…? • Based on what you know, how would you explain…? • How would you justify…? • What evidence can be used to support the opinion…?

Figure 12: Bloom's Taxonomy of Critical Thinking Skills continuum (Hopkins & Craig, 2015)

Chapter reflection questions

After reading chapter 4, take a moment to reflect on your learning and understanding.

1. How might thinking routines support the development of student thinking?
2. Why is it important to recognise the phases of development when utilising thinking routines?
3. Think about the thinking routine See Think Wonder. What phase of development are you at with using this routine? What phase of development are your students at?
4. How will you support the development of thinking with thinking routines?
5. What role does questioning currently play in your classroom?
6. How can we enhance the use of questioning in the classroom?

CHAPTER 5

Planning for critical and creative thinking in the classroom

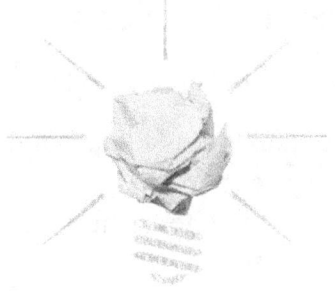

"Our goals can only be reached through a vehicle of a plan, in which we must fervently believe, and upon which we must vigorously act. There is no other route to success"

Pablo Picasso

It might seem contradictory to explicitly plan for thinking, but it is essential that teachers are intentional about their use of pedagogical strategies, in the critical and creative thinking space, to support student learning. As all educators know, there are many facets that need to be considered when planning for learning. These plans become the blueprint that shapes the what, when, how and why of learning. If we are to be strategic and explicit in our modelling, scaffolding and promotion of critical and creative thinking, then we need to strategically plan for it.

This chapter explores how teachers can work through the planning process to intentionally and explicitly scaffold the thinking of students. It draws upon the Australian Professional Standards for Teachers to shape the discussion around the planning process and highlights pictures of practice from my own teaching experience to paint a picture for how teachers might approach planning for critical and creative thinking in the classroom (NSW Education Standards Authority, 2018).

Chapter learning intentions

By the end of this chapter, educators will be able to:

- Utilise the Australian Professional Standards for Teachers in the planning cycle
- Understand ways to plan for critical and creative thinking

Australian Professional Standards for Teachers

The NSW Education Standards Authority (NESA) released the Australian Professional Standards for Teachers in 2014, with a revised edition later released in 2018. It comprises seven standards that outline what teachers should know and be able to do. These standards are interconnected, interdependent and overlapping. They are grouped into three domains of teaching: Professional knowledge, professional practice and professional engagement. In practice, teaching draws on aspects of all three domains. Effective practitioners use the standards to shape the work that they do, and the planning phase is no different.

DOMAINS OF TEACHING	STANDARDS
Professional knowledge	1. Know students and how they learn 2. Know the content and how to teach it
Professional practice	3. Plan for and implement effective teaching and learning 4. Create and maintain supportvie and safe learning environments 5. Assess, provide feedback and report on student learning
Professional engagement	6. Engage in professional learning 7. Engage professionally with colleagues, parents/carers and the community

Figure 13: Australian Professional Standards for Teachers (NSW Education Standards Authority, 2018)

Professional knowledge: Know the content and how to teach it

As educators, we should know the syllabus documents we teach, the outcomes and content descriptors embedded within the syllabus like the backs of our hands. These documents provide the platform for learning in the classroom and detail the 'what' component of teaching. Critical and creative thinking is embedded as a general capability across the syllabus documents and is generally indicated by the use of a 'cog-like symbol'. When we begin the planning process, this is where we begin. There are a number of key questions and steps that educators follow when they begin to frame learning.

Syllabus and links

When beginning the planning process, start by examining the syllabus outcomes and content descriptors. These signal to educators what students must know and be able to do. Think about:

- What outcomes do I need to address in this learning cycle?
- What are the cross-curriculum priorities and general capabilities addressed in this unit?
- What opportunities are there for harnessing other key learning areas to build a broader picture of learning and concept knowledge?

The verbs used in outcomes and descriptors provide the keys for educators to know the type of thinking they will require a student to demonstrate. Highlight the verbs and note down what this verb will require.

Knowledge, understanding and skills
The development of students' thought processes grounded in content makes it clear to all that the act of thinking and the development of critical and creative thinking is not a stand-alone skill, but something that underpins and is taught through the content in all curriculum areas and across all grades and stages. Think about:

- What key content do I want my students to know and understand?
- What skills do I want them to be able to demonstrate?
- How will the development of critical and creative thinking be grounded in this content?
- What supports and scaffolds will my students need to engage with, think about, question and reflect on this learning?

Assessment
Assessment forms a vital part of the learning process. This is where we make judgements about learning growth and achievement of our students. It is important to remember that assessment comes in many forms: *Assessment For, As and Of Learning*. Think about:

- How will I use assessment for, as and of learning throughout the teaching and learning cycle to gauge student understanding and development of thinking?
- What products of learning will be used to assess knowledge, understanding, skills and thinking?
- How will I promote the process as an important part of the product of learning?
- How will I know students have achieved the outcomes?
- How will students know they have achieved the learning intention and success criteria?

Feedback and feed forward

The most powerful and effective learning experiences are those that embed feedback and feed forward into the process. Too often this is the component that falls by the wayside when time is critical, however, it is a practice that educators need to elevate. Feedback is about supporting students to understand how their learning is travelling in relation to the success criteria. Feed forward is about providing students clear and succinct steps to move learning forward in order to achieve success.

Providing time for feedback and feed forward doesn't need to be undertaken at the end of a lesson. It could simply be provided as the students engage with the learning process. What is certain is that feedback provided without the student in attendance and after the learning has been completed has very little impact on student growth and attainment. Think about:

- What feedback and feed forward will be given during the different phases of the learning cycle?
- How will I ensure my feedback and feed forward links to the success criteria and learning intention for the lesson?
- How can I promote self-regulation through feedback?

Professional practice: Plan for and implement effective teaching and learning

Choosing the right type of 'tool' for the job is something builders are all too familiar with. As educators, we need to be intentional with the types of questions, thinking routines, processes and practices we are employing in our classrooms on a daily basis. It is not enough to leave it to chance.

When we are planning, using a lesson or unit template, teachers need to identify the specific scaffold and questioning prompts they will explicitly teach students to support their understanding. Take, for example, figure 14 below that snapshots a section of my teaching and learning programme for Stage 3 History.

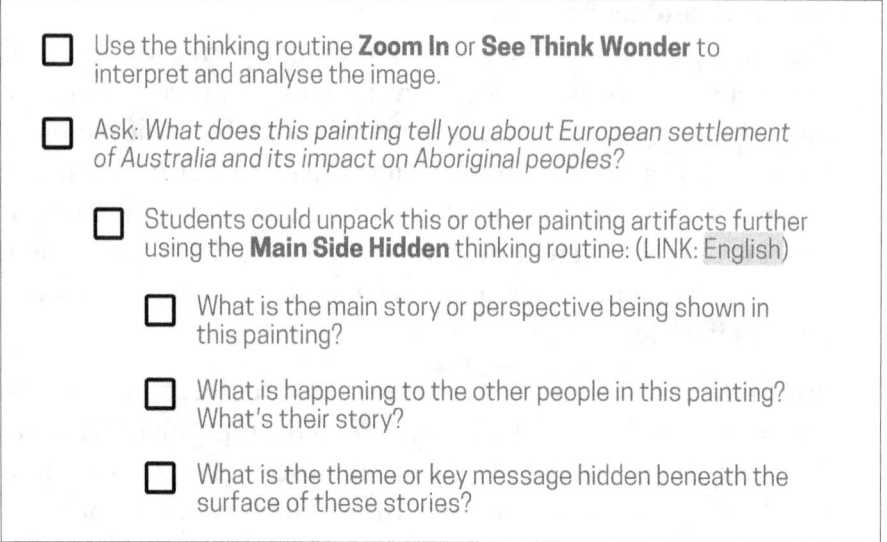

Figure 14: Zoom In programme snapshot

Here's what you may have noticed:

- The first point highlights the thinking routine I want to use to support students: Zoom In and a possibility of using the See Think Wonder routine.
- Specific identification of the thinking skills students need to utilise: **interpreting** and **analysing**.
- The context is a historical artwork.
- The second point highlights further support as students use the information they interpreted and analysed from the artwork in point one to answer the question in point two.
- There are links between the historical component and other key curriculum areas.

The Zoom In thinking routine (Ritchhart et al, 2011) is a great way to support students as they observe gradual portions of an image closely. This allows students to interpret sections of the image in manageable chunks before revealing the entire image to the students. This routine also allows teachers to support students in developing an understanding of inferencing as they use visual context clues to make sense of the artwork. Combining the Zoom In thinking routine with the See Think Wonder routine allows teachers to scaffold the discussion around the image, especially if, like my class, this is the first time they are engaging with this type of learning and utilising these thought processes in this way.

Scan the QR code to find out more about the Zoom In thinking routine.

Take a look now to see how this portion of planning translates into the classroom. What you will observe is a series of slide decks that break down the thought processes to help the students formulate ideas and interpret the image. Each prompt on the slide is presented to students individually as I use the Zoom In thinking routine combined with the See Think Wonder and What Makes You Say That routines. As this was the students' first introduction to using the Zoom In routine, the task was explicitly modelled and scaffolded.

The students in my class were well versed in using the See Think Wonder routine, working at an advanced phase. This familiarity with the routine allowed them to draw on these embedded skills and apply it to a new routine and situation. Students examined the historical painting *Thomas Baines with Aborigines near the mouth of the Victoria River*, NT circa 1857 from the National Library of Australia.

> **Zoom In...**
>
> What do you see, observe or notice?
>
> What do you think might be occurring in this painting?
>
> What makes you say that?
>
> What do you wonder?

Figure 15: Zoom In part I

Part I, as seen in figure 15, shows the portion of image the students engaged with alongside the scaffolded questions used to help them to observe, interpret and analyse the historical artifact. The question *What do you see, observe or notice?* asks students to focus purely on the facts of what can be seen. Asking students about their thoughts on what is happening through the prompt *What do you think might be occurring in this painting?* allows students to bring their background knowledge in order to draw inferences about the possibilities. The prompt *What makes you say that?* asks students to justify their interpretations and inferences based on the facts at hand and their prior knowledge. Ending part I with the wondering prompt *What do you wonder?* allows students to ask questions about the artifact, where the information presented doesn't yet connect to their prior knowledge and understanding.

Figure 16: Zoom In part II

Part II, as seen in figure 16, shows the new information revealed to the students and how the types of questions change to support students to build on the interpretations they have already made. Through the types of question prompts I chose, the third question *Has the new information changed any of your wonders or changed your thinking?* brings in an element of reflection. Although the question is a closed question, further prompting through asking students to elaborate draws out the reflective component of this question prompt.

Figure 17: Zoom In part III

Part III, as seen in figure 17, highlights how the question prompts shift slightly with the full painting reveal. By this point, the students have engaged with the components of the image and several question prompts to support the interpretation and analysis of the historical artifact. Engaging with the Zoom In routine in this way helps students to achieve the next phase of learning, which is to be able to use their interpretations and analysis to build explanations and draw conclusions about the historical painting and the importance of the message it portrays.

What does this painting tell you about European settlement of Australia and its impact on Aboriginal peoples?

What is the main story or perspective being shown in this painting?

What is happening to the other people in this painting? What is their story?

What is the theme or key message hidden beneath the surface of these stories?

Figure 18: Zoom In meets Main Side Hidden

The Zoom In meets Main Side Hidden routine, as seen in figure 18, highlights the importance of utilising the Zoom In routine to build the base for students to interpret and analyse a painting. It is the springboard from which students are then supported to answer the big historical question. Without utilising the thinking routine, explicitly teaching students to think in a particular way and using it as a rich learning platform, solely answering the historical question would not have yielded the same rich discussions, development of knowledge and thinking.

It is therefore important that educators recognise opportunities where it is important to 'go slow in order to go deep' and chunk the learning in order to make greater educational gains. What is also important here, and something I haven't yet mentioned, is the documentation of thinking and discussion as both students and teachers engage with the thinking routine. For a multifaceted routine like Zoom In, it is important to capture the student thinking throughout the process.

This could be individually recorded by students or collaboratively in small groups or as a whole class. The way you document the process depends entirely on the purpose of using the routine in relation to the content and what the teacher will then do with the documented evidence. Think about:

- What is it I want my students to be able to do by the end of the lesson or series of lessons?
- How will scaffolding the thinking process benefit all learners?
- Which thinking routine is going to provide the best scaffolding?
- How will I model my own thinking throughout the process?

Professional practice: Assess, provide feedback and report on student learning

One of the benefits to explicitly using thinking routines to scaffold and support students' metacognitive processes is that it allows educators to pinpoint areas for further development. This allows teachers the opportunity to provide additional support in the development of that thinking skill so that students can be successful in their learning – this provides a rich opportunity to also provide meaningful and timely feedback and feed forward. Think back to the Zoom In thinking routine. To utilise the routine as part of the assessment for the learning process, look for how students:

- Pay attention to detail and how they support their assumptions by referring to what they have seen and noticed.
- Are students synthesising the new information as it is provided to them to develop new or modified predictions and interpretations?
- Do students build on the ideas of others, or do they limit their thinking only to their ideas?
- Are they able to reflect on how and why their thinking has changed throughout the process?

Thinking about and answering questions like these as part of the formative assessment process provides powerful observations about student learning and the impact of a thinking routine on the outcome of learning.

Planning for thinking in a remote learning environment

The past few years in education have been interesting, to say the least. Teachers around the globe have had to navigate years of a global pandemic and numerous lockdowns, making educating our students that much more complex. A lockdown does not mean that we put the development of critical and creative thinking on the backburner. In a time of great uncertainty, students need routine and certainty. Continuing to develop critical and creative thinking through the continued use of thinking routines, questioning prompts, explicit teaching (virtually) and the gradual release of responsibility is as important now as it is or was when educators could teach face to face in the classroom.

It is through the integration of technology that we continue to embed critical and creative thinking skills in the learning that is occurring. There is an abundance of applications out there that can help teachers achieve this. For example:

- **Seesaw Plus** – this application allows teachers to upload a thinking routine template for students to share their thinking. This allows teachers to actively promote the thinking of students in order to make it visible and valued. Teachers are able to provide written and verbal feedback to students about their learning, engaging parents also in the process.

- **Google Classroom** – this versatile tool can be used to share thinking routine templates individually or collaboratively as a means to documenting the thought processes of students and using it as an ongoing artifact of learning and reflective tool.

- **Flipgrid** – this application is useful for capturing audio and visual evidence of thinking without the real need to provide written evidence. It provides short, sharp, audio responses to a question prompt or thinking routine.

- **Videoconferencing** – platforms such as Zoom or Microsoft Teams help teachers to be able to continue the development of students' critical and creative thinking skills in a virtual space. These are great tools to support collaborative thinking through breakout rooms or through collaborative tasks.

Regardless of the technology tools and applications you have available to you, the integration of thinking routines is a simple way that we can continue to build student thinking capabilities and continue to foster a thinking classroom. Take, for instance, the Tug of War thinking routine (Ritchhart et al, 2011). This routine is great for helping learners to understand the complexity of a dilemma and consider various factors in the decision-making process. It is a thinking routine that is comprised of a number of key components:

- Identifying and framing the opposing sides
- Generating as many reasons as possible that pull you towards
- Determining the strength of each tug – placing the strongest reasons at the furthest ends
- Capturing any 'what if' questions

During lockdown periods in Australia, lots of discussions were being had about the 'fairness' of different restrictions imposed on our lives. To help students make sense of these and consider all points of view and perspectives on the matter, we used the Tug of War thinking routine in the virtual space to discuss and unpack these. Students in Years 5 and 6 were provided the topic for discussion prior to the virtual check-in session and were asked to consider the factors around it.

As we gathered to discuss the topic in a videoconferencing application, we also utilised an application that could capture the 'pull factors' and allow us to sort and manipulate them as the discussion unfolded, such as the application Jamboard. The use of technology supported students to remain connected, and to continue to develop their critical and creative thinking skills in a virtual environment. The adaptability and flexibility of thinking routines means that a focus on building a thinking classroom did not have to cease simply because online learning was now the new norm.

Figure 19: Tug of War thinking routine (Ritchhart et al, 2011)

Scan the QR code to find out more about the Tug of War thinking routine.

Chapter reflection questions

After reading chapter 5, take a moment to reflect on your learning and understanding.

1. How do the Australian Professional Standards for Teachers support the planning phase of learning?
2. Think about the descriptors in Standard 3 and highlight the key verbs. Highlight where you are now and what you need to do to move to the next level. List down the verbs you need to be able to demonstrate in your teaching and learning moving forward.
3. How will you achieve this goal?
4. Why is it important to explicitly plan for and utilise thinking routines in the classroom?

PART THREE

THE THINKING CLASSROOM IN ACTION

CHAPTER 6

Critical and creative thinking in literacy

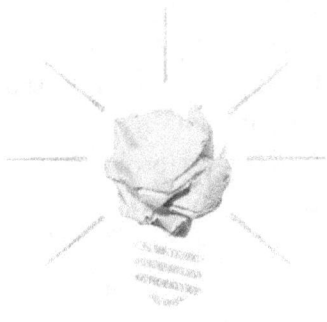

"Activating thinking in concert with literacy skills can lead to deeper thinking. Reading, writing, speaking and listening are interconnected skills that are key to facilitating thinking"

Stobaugh and Love (2021)

Literacy is the foundation on which we hinge all other learning. It forms an integral part of the curriculum across Australia. Embedding thinking routines into literacy practices is a powerful way to support students as they learn to understand the complex nature of the English language and apply it to other disciplines across the curriculum.

This chapter provides a snapshot of a number of thinking routines that explore practical examples and ideas on ways teachers can embed thinking routines and other critical and creative thinking practices in the literacy classroom. It examines the purpose of specific routines, how to utilise them in the classroom and puzzles of practice from the classroom. This chapter will explore four thinking routines from the work of Ritchhart and colleagues (2011), including See Think Wonder, Main Side Hidden, Step Inside and Peel the Fruit.

Chapter learning intentions

By the end of this chapter, educators will be able to:

- Identify a range of thinking routines
- Explain how thinking routines support and scaffold student thinking in literacy
- Reflect on and explore the implications on their own classroom practice

See Think Wonder

In every classroom, no matter what age, I can guarantee that students will be examining and discussing a range of different stimuli, including images, digital media, provocations, quality texts or literature and more. When educators present students with a stimulus, there is generally a number of things we want students to do with that stimuli, such as notice, wonder, interpret, infer, analyse, explain, justify, describe or identify. More often than not, educators combine a couple of these key verbs together to unpack the stimuli, but in doing so, we are asking students to draw on different thinking moves to unpack an image, quality text or provocation, etc. Strategically utilising a thinking routine can support students to navigate this process and unlock the key metacognitive processes they require to engage with the learning experience.

The thinking routine See Think Wonder (Ritchhart et al, 2011) is one of the first routines I introduce to students to help them unpack their thinking and wonderings about different stimuli. It is a highly versatile routine that works really well with visual images, short clips, artifacts, patterns, small texts or picture books. This routine fosters the thinking moves of wondering, describing what's there, building explanations and reasoning with evidence. These thinking moves help students to make careful observations and begin to make predictions and conclusions based on current evidence and understanding.

When engaging students with this routine, I utilise the three prompts:

- What do you see, observe or notice?
- What does it make you think?
- What do you wonder?

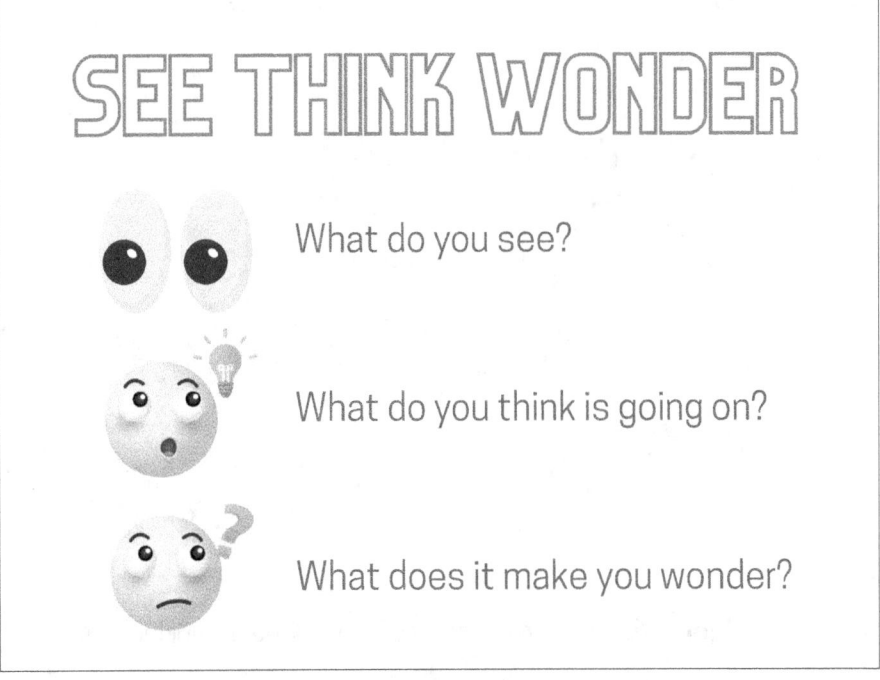

Figure 20: See Think Wonder thinking routine
(adapted from Ritchhart et al, 2011)

In the initial phase of development, this routine is highly structured, beginning with asking students to list all the things they can see, before moving to what they think about what they are seeing and finally recording any wonderings they might have about the stimulus. As this routine is used on a regular basis, both teachers and students become more comfortable with it and are able to apply it to a variety of different content areas. Moving along the phases of development continuum means that less teacher scaffolding is required until students are able to use it seamlessly.

Take, for instance, the use of the See Think Wonder thinking routine with Year 5 students using the quality text *Fire* by author Jacki French. This text was used in a Year 5 Geography unit as a way for students to explore and develop their understanding of bushfires and utilise their literacy skills to describe a bushfire through the development of poetic text. Before engaging with the thinking routine, we read through the text as a class. After listening to a reading of the text, the students were given a copy of the words from the text. It is here that we engaged the thinking routine See Think Wonder to support students as I asked them to unpack the text in a particular way.

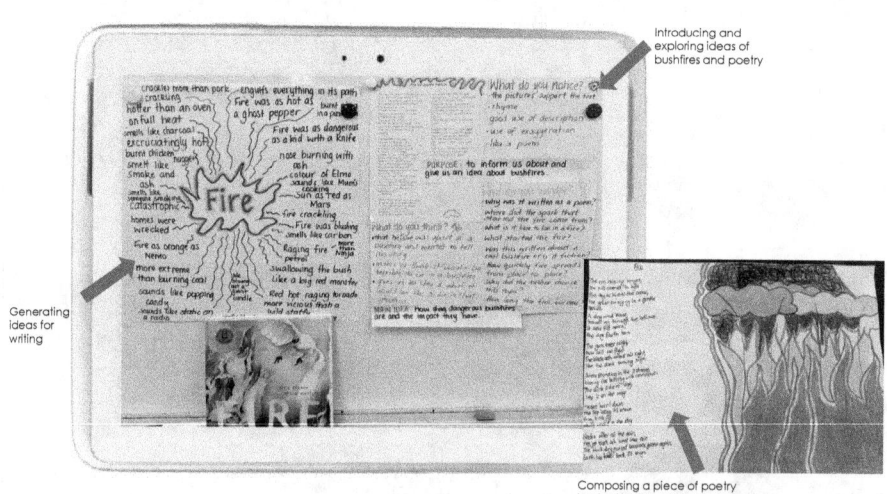

Figure 21: Example of the See Think Wonder thinking routine in action

Prompt 1: What do you see?
This prompt asks students to identify the things they notice about the text. The wording of the question focuses thinking purely on the facts. It is here that students identify particular things about the text, such as text structure, text features, use of vocabulary, figurative and descriptive language, and the role the images play in supporting the text. It was at this point that students were able to identify how this text was similar to other poetry we had previously explored and justify what the connections were. This helped to set the scene for building our learning towards the development of our own poetic pieces about bushfires.

Prompt 2: What do you think?
This prompt asks students to bring in a layer of inference supported by the key details present in the text. For this particular part of the thinking routine, I adapted the questions slightly and posed *What do you think this text is telling us?* Adapting the prompt slightly allowed me to focus the students' attention on the purpose of the text as well as identifying the main idea. The later skill is often one we know students find difficult when examining data such as NAPLAN assessment data.

Prompt 3: What do you wonder?
The final prompt is about exploring the wonderings that have arisen through the unpacking of the stimulus. For the students in my Year 5 class, this allowed them to ask clarifying questions of the text to clear up any uncertainties they had about key ideas or themes. It also provided them with an opportunity to ask questions that stemmed from the text, but were not directly or indirectly stated in the text, such as *Was this written about a real bushfire or experience with a real bushfire?* What we discovered was that many of the questions we couldn't explicitly answer, so we set out to connect with the author to help us build a greater understanding about why they wrote the text, what experience they had with the topic and their reasoning for writing the text in that particular way.

This provided the perfect platform on which to springboard off and begin generating ideas and composing our own poetic texts about bushfires. What was written by the students about the topic was powerful and something they were immensely proud of. If I had just given my students the task of writing about a bushfire without the appropriate scaffolding and prompting, I am certain I would not have received the same depth in student writing from *all* of my students.

Adapting the routine

Making adaptations to the way you prompt through questioning when using the See Think Wonder routine is not difficult. What needs to be considered is the type of prompt or stimulus being used, the type of thinking you are trying to illicit and the end learning goal you want students to achieve. For example, here are some ways that I adapt the prompts:

- **SEE**
  - What do you see, observe or notice?
- **THINK**
  - What does it make you think will happen?
  - Why do you think this occurred?
  - What does the image make you think?
- **WONDER**
  - What does it make you wonder?
  - What questions do you have?

Personally, I like to add observing and noticing to the 'see' prompt as it builds students' observational language. As the students become more comfortable with the routine, I find that they begin to use the language of this prompt in classroom discussions.

Scan the QR code to find out more about the See Think Wonder thinking routine.

Main Side Hidden

How often do we examine a piece of literature, an image or event from the perspective of the main person or people involved or affected? From a young age, we teach our children to comprehend and analyse stories from the point of view of the main character. We view images, photographs, artifacts and events from the more prominent point of view. Think back to the last piece of literature, image or event you explored with your students. Through what lens was this stimulus viewed? Were there opportunities for students to explore the other stories that were present that may or may not be deemed of lesser importance in the big scheme of things?

Being able to effectively explore the multiple narratives that are present in literature, images and events can be a tricky skill for learners to master. We want our students to be able to examine things from different perspectives and alternative points of view to discern bias and develop a more balanced take on issues, ideas and events. Not to mention developing empathy for 'the other'.

The Project Zero thinking routine (Ritchhart et al, 2011) Main Side Hidden is a perfect tool that educators can strategically employ to help students learn how to effectively examine the different perspectives that occur when multiple narratives are present. It is a great routine for helping students understand how supporting characters help to move a narrative along but also have stories in their own rights.

In the initial phases of development this routine is highly structured, but as the routine is used on a regular basis across all key learning areas, the students are able to use it and apply it seamlessly. Take, for instance, the examination of the fairy tale *Cinderella*. This is a well-known story told to generations of children, and one that the majority of my students knew extremely well. This text provided a great springboard for helping students learn to dig deeper into the text and look at what else was going on.

Figure 22: Main Side Hidden thinking routine (Ritchhart et al, 2011)

I used the following prompts to help scaffold student thinking, which were adapted from Ritchhart et al (2011):

- What is happening to the main character(s) in the story?
- What is happening to the other characters in the story? What is their story?
- What is the theme or key message that is hidden beneath the surface of these stories?

Prompt 1: What is happening to the main character in the story?
This prompt requires students to first determine the main person or people in the narrative being told. It requires them to identify the actions, emotions and events that occur in the story for each of these characters – or character if there is only one. This prompt also presents a great opportunity for students to gather clues from the text that help them highlight the emotions or actions taken by the particular character and support their statements.

When using this prompt with my students and the text *Cinderella*, I found they were quite adept at highlighting the main character and identifying the story, actions and emotions that encapsulate her. Beginning with a known stimulus ensured that my students were able to build on what they knew.

Prompt 2: What is happening to the other characters in the story? What is their story?

As with the first prompt, students need to identify the other characters that form part of the narrative(s) being examined, and explore the actions, emotions and events that are being told on the side. These stories may or may not include the direct involvement of the main character(s). This prompt also affords students the opportunity to pose questions about 'why' and make inferences about the actions, emotions and events that these other characters feature in.

This prompt saw my students enthralled in the story of the mean stepmother. They initially began by describing her qualities based on their previous understanding of her, but as the discussion evolved students began to question the actions of the stepmother. "*What if she had been mistreated at a young age so she now does the same to Cinderella?*" or "*Does she actually like Cinderella, but doesn't want to make her daughters jealous?*" These were just some of the interesting questions posed and unpacked by my 5th grade students.

Prompt 3: What is the theme or key message that is hidden beneath the surface of these stories?

This prompt requires students to determine the theme or key message the author is trying to portray to their audience. This prompt also presents opportunities to gather evidence to support their claim for particular themes arising from a text. When we stood back and examined the vast range of stories present in the fairy tale *Cinderella*, we began to see that there were some patterns in behaviour and actions from the characters and themes that were emerging.

So, where to next?

We used the Main Side Hidden thinking routine as the strategic platform from which to explore multiple perspectives in a text and then used these perspectives to compose an imaginative paragraph of writing from one of the character's points of view.

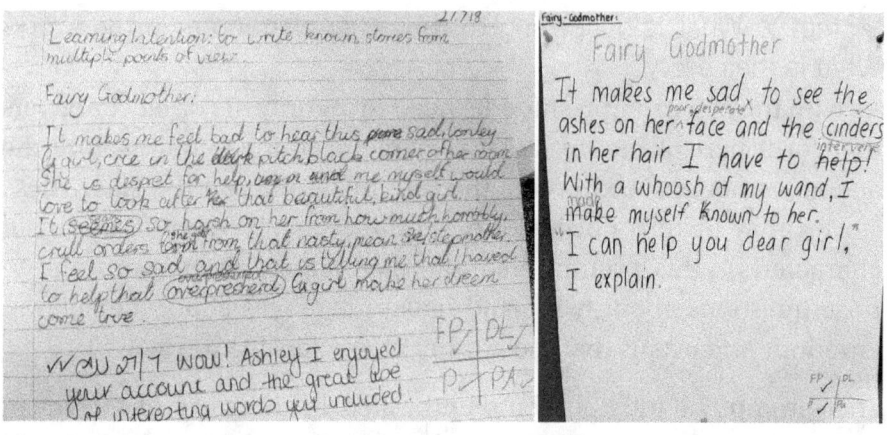

Figure 23: Main Side Hidden examples

Adapting the thinking routine

Making adaptations to the way you prompt through questioning when using the Main Side Hidden routine is not difficult. What needs to be considered is the age of the learner, and the type of thinking and response you are wanting students to consider. For example, here are some ways that I adapt the prompts:

- **MAIN**
    - Who is the main character? What is the main story being told?
- **SIDE**
    - What is happening to the other characters in the story? What is their story?
- **HIDDEN**
    - What is the theme or key message hidden beneath the surface of these stories?

Prior to using this thinking routine, students need to have a strong understanding of what a theme or key message is, in order to engage independently with this routine. It is important that educators spend time modelling and scaffolding this routine in order to unlock the thinking routine's true potential for learners.

Scan the QR code to find out more about the Main Side Hidden thinking routine.

Step Inside

Examining how an author develops a character over the course of a text, exploring the personality traits, actions and the way they handle different situations that they are faced with in the text is a complex skill educators ask students to engage with at varying levels. It can be a difficult skill for students to master, but the use of the Step Inside thinking routine (Ritchhart et al, 2011) is a valuable routine that educators can utilise to model, scaffold and support students through the thinking moves required to achieve success with this notoriously difficult skill.

This routine fosters the thinking moves of describing what's there, wondering, building explanations, considering different viewpoints and reasoning with evidence. These thinking moves help students to view a place, people, situations, events or things through different lenses and points of view, and it opens up possibilities for creating, for example, a written piece. This thinking routine utilises four supporting questions to help scaffold and support student thinking:

- What can this person or thing see, observe or notice?
- What might the person or thing know, understand, hold true or believe?

- What might the person or thing care deeply about?
- What might the person or thing wonder about or question?

STEP INSIDE

What can this person or thing see, observe or notice?

What might the person or thing know, understand, hold true or believe?

What might the person or thing care deeply about?

What might the person or thing wonder about or question?

Figure 24: Step Inside thinking routine (adapted from Ritchhart et al, 2011)

Adapting the routine

When I engage students with this routine, I adapt the questioning prompts slightly to account for the language we use with our students in my context. The adapted questioning prompts I use are:

- What might this character see, observe or notice?
- What might this character think, understand or believe?
- What does this character care deeply about?
- What might this character be wondering?

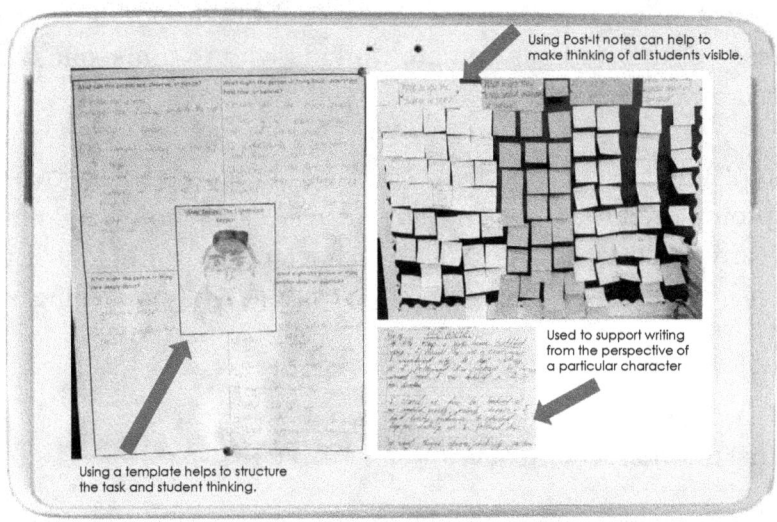

Figure 25: Step Inside thinking routine example

Here are a couple of examples of how I have utilised the thinking routine with students to support and develop their thinking using stimuli such as an animation and quality literature in order to springboard into the writing process. When introducing this routine to students, I explicitly guide them through each step initially modelling my own thinking alongside the students'. Utilising thinking routine templates or Post-it notes is one way I provide a scaffold to students. As students use the routine more and become more comfortable with it, I gradually release the responsibility to undertake tasks that draw on the Step Inside thinking routine independently.

Prompt 1: What might this character see, observe or notice?
This prompt asks students to identify the things that they notice and observe. It is a prompt that is grounded in the identification of facts. When connecting this prompt with a text or animation, students record the things that they can visually see or through what is written on the page. Focusing purely on the facts helps students to examine what is there without needing to draw on the skill of inferencing just yet. If students are familiar with other routines that utilise this prompt, they may feel comfortable working with this prompt without a great

deal of scaffolding required; however, it is always important to gauge the needs of the students you are working with to understand what their learning needs are.

Prompt 2: What might this character think, understand or believe?

This prompt requires deeper thought processes from students as they learn to take the facts about a character and combine that with inferencing skills in order to draw conclusions about three things:

- What the character thinks
- What the character understands
- What the character believes

As the educator, you may focus on one of these or all three. This is dependent on your learners and the overall purpose for asking the prompt. Reasoning with evidence based on information directly stated or implied in the text supports this component of the thinking routine. Utilising the additional prompt *What makes you say that?* can assist students as they learn to explain their thinking. The language and prior understanding about what the vocabulary in the question means could be a barrier for some students, and therefore additional learning is required around the terminology used.

Prompt 3: What does this character care deeply about?

This prompt asks students to draw on the previous two prompts to consider what a character may or may not care deeply about. This is a complex skill that again requires an understanding of the facts, the ability to read between the lines and make informed conclusions about a character. Out of the four prompts in this routine, this is possibly the component that requires the greatest explicit instruction, modelling, scaffolding and support.

Prompt 4: What might this character be wondering?

The final prompt in the Step Inside thinking routine is centred on wonderings. However, instead of drawing on the wonderings of the student, this prompt asks students to think about the kinds of questions the chosen character might be thinking or asking. Probing deeper through utilising additional questioning techniques will allow educators to uncover the level of understanding the student has about the text and the character at a greater level. This provides educators with a greater understanding of the comprehension ability of students and highlights any misconceptions a student may hold.

Scan the QR code to find out more about the Step Inside thinking routine.

Peel the Fruit

One of my favourite character exchanges in the movie *Shrek*, is when Shrek says to Donkey, "Onions have layers." How often do we ask students to examine a piece of quality literature in a range of ways and get frustrated when we ask students to examine different viewpoints or identify the central message only to be provided with mediocre responses? The good news is that analysing a text through the thinking routine Peel the Fruit (Ritchhart et al, 2020) can support this process in a structured way.

When I utilise the thinking routine Peel the Fruit with my students, I explain that this routine is like peeling back the layers until we get to the core or heart of the stimuli. This routine combines a range of thinking processes that require careful scaffolding as students move from lower-level cognitive skills through to more complex cognitive skills. It is a routine that has a large number of steps that increase in complexity and skill as you engage further with the routine.

- What do you see, observe or notice?
- What questions or puzzles do you have?
- What is this really about?
- How does this story fit with your life?
- How could we see this from another perspective?
- What is the central idea or message?

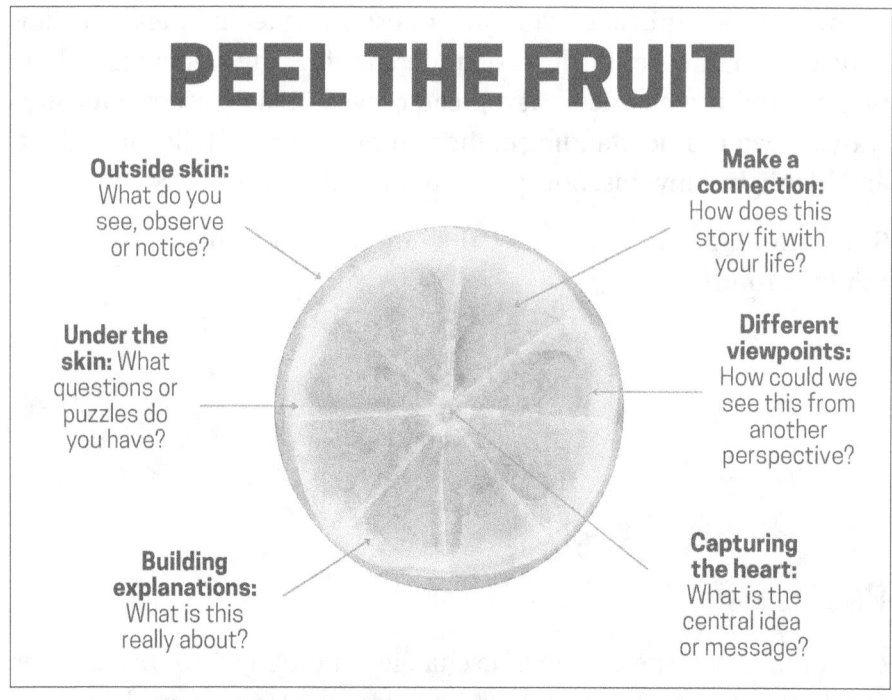

Figure 26: Peel the Fruit thinking routine (adapted from Ritchhart, 2020)

You may have noticed that the first couple of prompts have appeared in two of the thinking routines we have already explored in this chapter. One of the reasons why thinking routines are valuable tools to make thinking visible in the classroom is because many of the routines draw on similar 'thinking moves'. This means that students can apply their metacognitive processes easily for that component without relying on too much cognitive processing to understand the type of thinking required. Here's an example of how I have utilised this routine in the classroom, using the text *The Story of Rosy Dock* by Jeannie Baker.

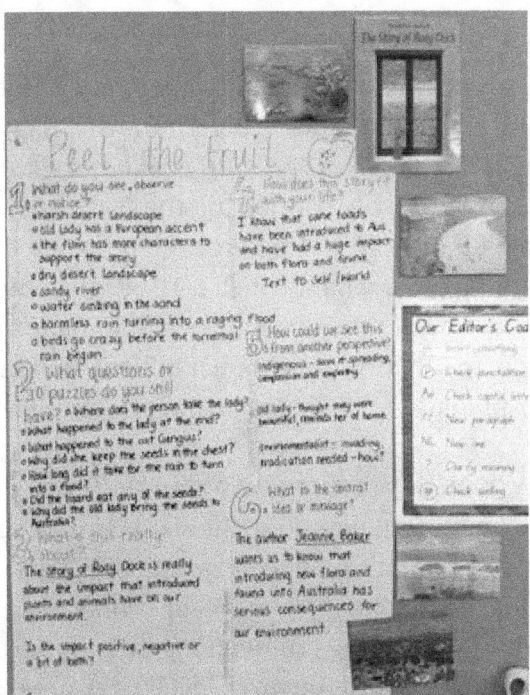

Figure 27: Peel the Fruit whole-class documentation example

Prompt 1: What do you see, observe or notice?
This prompt starts by asking students to identify what can be visually seen through images or text, through asking *What do you see?* or *What do you see, observe or notice?* It helps students to focus on the facts at hand without drawing on the skills of inferencing or beginning to make judgements about why. If students have been exposed to this prompt through engaging with other routines, they will find this prompt very familiar. When using this prompt with Year 6 students, they identified what they could see in the text in terms of key phrases and visual images.

Prompt 2: What questions or puzzles do you have?
This prompt asks students to think about their wonderings related to the text, through asking *What do you wonder?* or *What questions or puzzles do you have?* It is through these questions that teachers can understand the depth of student thinking about the text as well as use the questions to drive learning and dive deeper into the text. This prompt is a prominent feature of many other routines and is one the students generally feel comfortable with as naturally curious beings.

Prompt 3: What is this really about?
This prompt is about building explanations, where students use factual information and contextual clues to determine the main idea of the text, through asking *What is this really about?* or *What is the main idea of this text?* This relies on students connecting the facts from prompt 1 with information they have inferred based on contextual clues to explain what is really going on or what the text is really all about. It is here that students require explicit modelling and scaffolding to support them to understand how to identify and connect information in order to make an informed explanation that draws on the evidence from the text.

Prompt 4: How does this story fit with your life?
This prompt is about understanding how this text or stimuli connects with the viewer or reader's own life experiences, through asking *How does this story fit with your life?* or *What connections can you make to the text?* When examining connections, it is important to support students as they understand the three levels of connections:

- **Connection to self** – How does the stimuli connect to personal experience?
- **Connection to text** – How does the stimuli connect to another stimulus you have read or seen?
- **Connection to world** – How does the stimuli connect to something happening in the world?

Many students can identify connections to a stimulus without too much scaffolding and prompting, but others may need a greater amount of scaffolding to look for connections. It is not necessary to ask students to make connections on all three levels, but rather to identify the strongest connection. As an educator, when I observe students who struggle to connect with the stimuli, it is often due to a lack of background knowledge. It is at this point that I would build in extra opportunities for students to develop knowledge that will further support their understanding of the text or stimuli.

Prompt 5: How could we see this from another perspective?
This prompt asks students to look at the text or stimuli not from the perspective of the main character, but to look through the lens of a supporting character to see how the narrative may look and change

from an alternative point of view, through asking *How could we see this from another perspective?* or *How might another character or person see this event? What's their point of view?* Looking at something from a perspective other than our own is a complex skill that will require ongoing modelling, scaffolding and experimenting to support students to develop this important skill over time. As an educator, combining this prompt with something like a hot-seat activity, where students pretend to play a particular character and an audience asks the characters questions relating to the stimulus, often helps students to 'get inside' the head of a person or character from a stimulus.

Prompt 6: What is the central idea or message?
This prompt is by far the most challenging of the six prompts in this routine for students. It asks students to dig down and draw on multiple pieces of information and skills to identify the central message or theme of the text or stimuli, through asking *What is the central idea or message?* or *What is the key theme?* Students will need to understand how to use contextual clues combined with their understanding of how different themes manifest across different stimuli. As you can imagine, this prompt is complex and requires educators to provide explicit instruction in identifying the key message and theme of a stimuli.

One of the most powerful things about using thinking routines in the literacy classroom is the rich formative assessment data educators can gather from students. Through observations and documented evidence using a thinking routine template, educators can use this to support them to make informed decisions about where students are at currently, where learning needs to go next, and additional instructions and supports that may be required for groups of students, as the discussion, learning and unpacking of a stimuli continues to deepen.

Scan the QR code to find out more about the Peel the Fruit thinking routine.

Chapter reflection questions

After reading chapter 6, take a moment to reflect on your learning and understanding.

1. How might you utilise these thinking routines in your classroom?
2. How do these routines help you to scaffold student thinking?
3. Choose one thinking routine to embed in your teaching and learning programme over the next month. Explicitly using it at least twice a week:
   a. Identify a range of opportunities to use the routine in English.
   b. Scaffold the students through each component of the prompts.
   c. What do you notice the first time you use the routine?
   d. What do you notice after two weeks of using the routine?
   e. What do you notice after one month of using the routine with your students?
   f. How did the thinking routine support the development of student thinking?
   g. What wonderings arose for you?
   h. What did you notice about how students articulated their thinking as they used the routine?

CHAPTER 7

Critical and creative thinking in numeracy

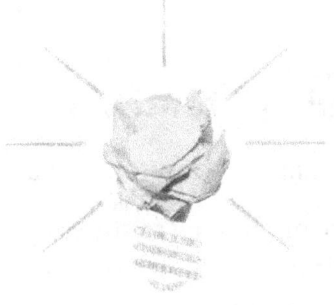

"A classroom culture that builds and extends students' thinking processes is central for effective learning"

ACARA

Numeracy is a foundational skill and a core curriculum area in Australia. Leveraging critical and creative thinking in the numeracy space supports students to see Mathematics as more than just learning a formula, but a vehicle through which to explore concepts, reveal patterns, question data and more. Creating a supportive and collaborative environment is essential if educators are to foster the development and application of thinking skills. The development of these thinking processes enables students to work mathematically and become effective problem-solvers (Sanders, 2016).

This chapter provides a snapshot of a number of thinking routines that explore practical examples and ideas on ways teachers can embed thinking routines and other critical and creative thinking practices in the numeracy classroom. It examines the purpose of specific routines, how to utilise them in the classroom and puzzles of practice from the classroom. This chapter will explore four thinking routines from the work of Ritchhart and colleagues (2011), including Claim Support Question, I used to think... Now I think..., See Think Wonder and Connect Extend Challenge.

Chapter learning intentions

By the end of this chapter, educators will be able to:

- Identify a range of thinking routines
- Explain how thinking routines support and scaffold student thinking in numeracy
- Reflect on and explore the implications on their own classroom practice

Claim Support Question

When we pose a claim or make a statement to students, how often do we help them scaffold their thinking in order to unpack what is really going on and delve deeper to find the truth? The thinking routine Claim Support Question (Ritchhart et al, 2011) is a routine that really encourages learners to dig deeper to identify and test the claims that we encounter during the exploration and investigation of learning. This routine is perfect for helping students to examine claims or statements closely and use evidence to support their thinking. This routine really helps students to reason with evidence, look at what is missing and identify contradictory information that disproves the claim or statement, allowing students to see things from both sides.

Figure 28: Claim Support Question
(adapted from Ritchhart et al, 2011)

When I first began using this thinking routine, I saw great possibilities for its use in the Mathematics classroom. We would examine statements and claims centred on mathematical concepts and elicit our prior knowledge and use current evidence to support or disprove the claims. Together with my learners, we navigated the initial phase of development for this routine. Early on I really grappled with ways to expand this routine beyond the subject area of Mathematics. I wanted to provide my learners with additional situations in which we could use this routine to scaffold our thinking in different ways, and to move beyond only using it in Mathematics. In order for this to occur, I needed to be comfortable with applying the routine across the strands of Mathematics.

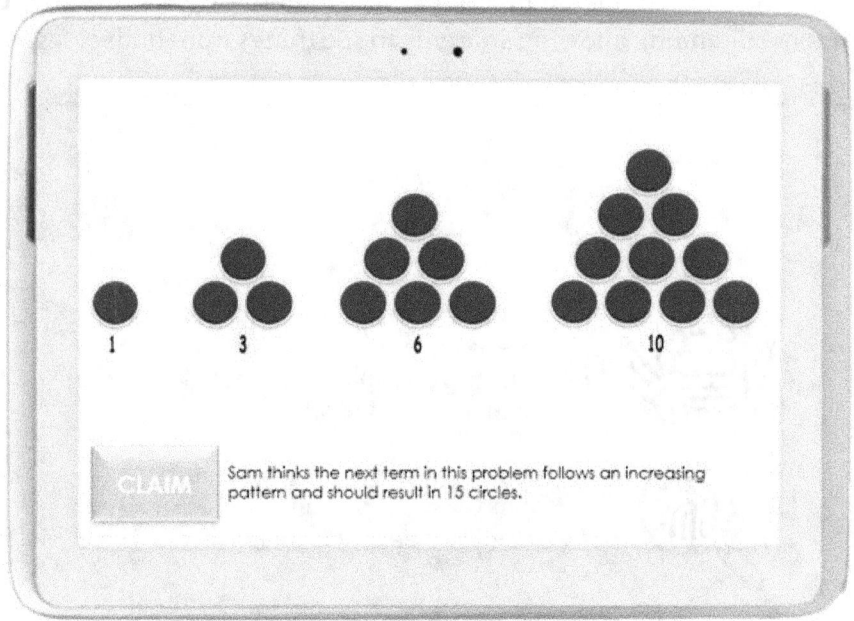

Figure 29: Claim Support Question example

Prompt 1: Claim
This prompt is a signal to students to identify the statement or claim to be examined or analysed through asking *What is the claim we are exploring?* It is in this crucial first step that teachers unpack the claim to be explored, utilising problem-solving strategies to understand what the claim is asking of students. Take, for instance, the claim in figure 29 Claim Support Question example. What information is important for students to know and understand in the claim? What strategies and concepts will be required to answer the claim?

Prompt 2: Support
This prompt is about exploring, investigating and analysing evidence that can be used to support the claim. In the Mathematics classroom, the use of manipulatives is an important part of helping students to

explore and tangibly experiment with a concept. It is at this point that students may also be asked to find evidence to disprove a claim or find discrepancies in the claim. The use of mathematical reasoning and discussion with peers will support students as they learn to support a claim.

Prompt 3: Question

This prompt asks students to raise questions relating to the claim being explored. Educators can support this through modelling what a curious learner looks and sounds like. For example, helping students to find gaps and ask questions such as *What is missing here? What am I not being told?* that might be used to support the statement being explored. This prompt really allows me to see what kinds of things the students are wondering as they move through and beyond the learning experience. More often than not these questions are used to help scaffold and drive our learning forward so that learning remains relevant, meaningful and authentic for students.

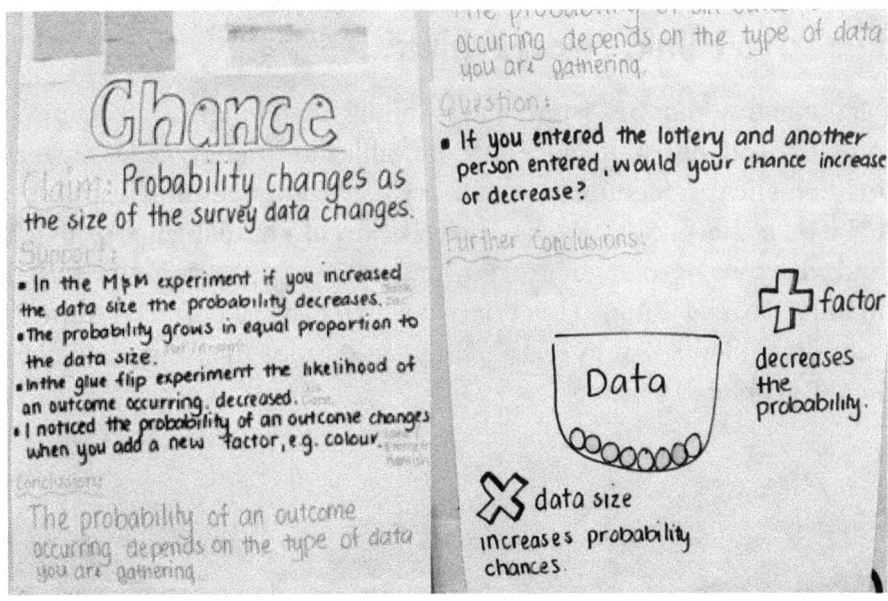

Figure 30: Claim Support Question whole-class documentation example

Here is another example of how I use the Claim Support Question in Mathematics. This example was undertaken with Year 6 students in the Mathematics strand of Statistics and Probability. The use of this routine to explore the probability of an outcome occurring in relation to the survey data size really helped to support students as they learnt to interrogate data and understand the role of probability. The use of the Claim Support Question routine allowed us to dive deeper into probability to really understand the role that data size has on the outcome and the interpretation of the preceding data.

Scan the QR code to find out more about the Claim Support Question thinking routine.

I used to think... Now I think...

Mathematics requires students to apply mathematical reasoning, problem-solving strategies and be able to identify the correct mathematical procedure. One of the crucial components of learning is to be reflective on what we have learnt, how our thinking has changed and where we need to go next as a learner. The thinking routine I used to think... Now I think... (Ritchhart et al, 2011) is the perfect routine to support students as they learn to build and refine the skills needed to be self-regulated learners.

Figure 31: I used to think... Now I think...
thinking routine (adapted from Ritchhart et al, 2011)

Prompt 1: I used to think

This prompt asks students to reflect on learning they have previously undertaken and consider how it has supported them to build on their prior knowledge in order to grow as a learner. As we share our thinking either in learning pods, as a class or individually with the teacher, I am always keen to find out what made them think this. This open conversation alone brings about rich discussions.

Prompt 2: Now I think

This prompt asks learners to think about and examine how their thinking has evolved over the learning process. I often ask students to elaborate on this response by adding 'because' or asking them how and/or why they know and understand this. This allows students to practise their ability to elaborate on their thinking and provide evidence to support their thinking.

Adapting the routine

A few years ago, I attended a Project Zero conference in Sydney. The keynote speaker at the conference was Rhonda Bondie, a researcher at Harvard, who talked about the value of this routine in helping students to reflect on their learning. However, she added that in order to help learners become self-regulated they need to continue the cycle beyond reflection. She suggested the prompt *So, next I will...* as a way to help students think about their next steps in the learning journey.

Prompt 3: So, next I will

This prompt allows students to forward plan and set learning goals as they move forward in the learning process, thus continuing the cycle of self-regulation. It also provides valuable insight to educators as to who has the ability to recognise their strengths and areas of improvement and who still needs to develop these skills.

In the numeracy classroom, I find this routine to be a perfect way to reflect on learning at the end of a lesson or a sequence of lessons. This routine makes for a great exit ticket and provides valuable insight for the teacher on the self-reflective capabilities of students and their ability to recognise how to take learning forward. This routine provides the perfect platform in which to support students to become self-reflective learners and to be able to articulate that to others. I often have students record their responses to this routine in their Mathematics book as a record of learning reflection and growth, as well as the opportunity to over time look back at where we were in Semester One and where we are now in Semester Two as we continue to build on our mathematical foundations and reasoning capabilities.

Scan the QR code to find out more about the I used to think... Now I think... thinking routine.

See Think Wonder

The thinking routine See Think Wonder is an extremely versatile routine and one that can be easily applied across the curriculum. We talked briefly about the components of the routine and a little about how to adapt the routine in chapter 6 (Critical and creative thinking in literacy). Here, we will look at how we can apply the same thinking routine to the Mathematics classroom. As previously mentioned, the See Think Wonder thinking routine helps learners to describe what is there, build explanations and develop wonderings to push learning forward.

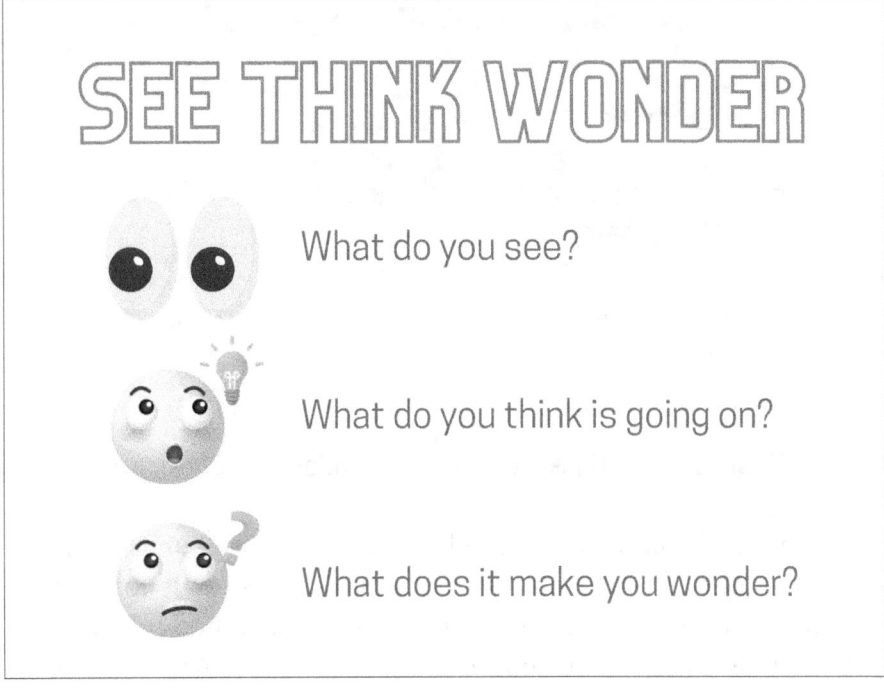

Figure 32: See Think Wonder thinking routine
(adapted from Ritchhart et al, 2011)

In my classroom, I use the thinking routine See Think Wonder on a regular basis to help students unpack their thinking about numbers, patterns and data being explored in Mathematics. Here are some examples of how I have drawn upon the routine with students in Year 5 and Year 6. What you will notice when you observe the examples is how the routine has been adapted to suit the content being examined and the purpose of utilising the routine to promote the thinking capabilities of students.

> Can we continue to create number patterns and describe how they are created?
>
>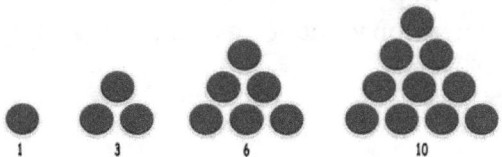
>
> What do you see, observe or notice?
>
> What does this make you think, in terms of how the pattern is created? How it is repeated?
>
> What questions or puzzles do you still have about these numbers?

Figure 33: See Think Wonder Mathematics prompt example

In this example, students engaged in a lesson focused on continuing, creating and describing number patterns. This example formed the beginning part of the lesson sequence as we examined how to work with number patterns and apply our thinking skills. You will also notice that this prompt uses the same pattern as the Claim Support Question example. This is to demonstrate how different thinking routines can be used with a single prompt to elicit different kinds of thinking and examine stimuli in particular ways depending upon the purpose and intent for learning.

Prompt 1: What do you see, observe or notice?
Through this prompt, I asked students to take time to observe the pattern and identify what they saw: numbers, groups of circles,

increasing numbers/circles. Once we listed the facts based on our observations, I shifted the discussion to using this information to build explanations about the pattern.

Prompt 2: What does this make you think?

Through this prompt, I adapted the question slightly to narrow it. This choice was taken in order to focus the discussion on our overarching intent for learning. I therefore posed the questions *What does this make you think, in terms of how the pattern is created? How is it repeated?* We utilised manipulatives to play around with the pattern, in order to be able to confidently explain how it was created, how it was repeated and what might appear next in the fifth term. By providing students with the time and space to explore their preconceived ideas about the pattern, apply mathematical reasoning and experiment with the pattern beyond what was observed allows the students to build confidence in investigating number patterns.

Prompt 3: What do you wonder?

Through this prompt, I provided students with the opportunity to question and pose problems or puzzles. I again adapted the prompt slightly to *What questions or puzzles do you still have about these numbers?* The discussions that stem from the questioning prompts often provide wonderful opportunities to dig deeper, apply mathematical reasoning and develop understanding.

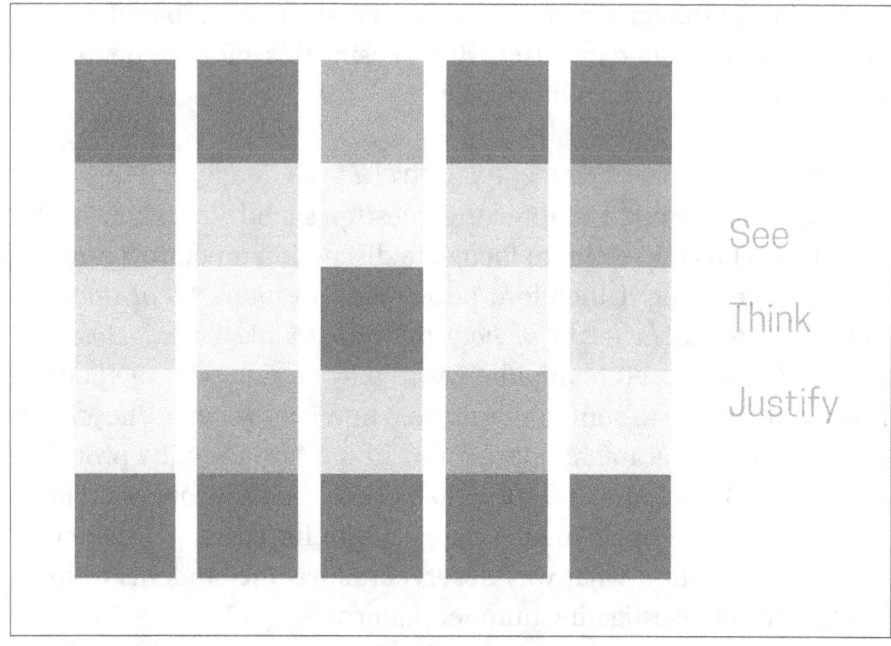

Figure 34: See Think Wonder Mathematics prompt example

In this example, students engaged in a lesson focused on exploring fractions, decimals and percentages through geometric art. At this point in the academic school year, students had been exposed to the See Think Wonder thinking routine in a range of other learning areas, such as in literacy, Visual Arts and the Humanities. This lesson linked their prior understanding of using the routine and supported students to apply the routine in the curriculum area of Mathematics. During this lesson, students were examining how fractions can be represented through geometric art.

Prompt 1: What do you see, observe or notice?
Through this prompt, students were asked to again make observations and provide facts about the image – blue (dark grey), red (grey), yellow (like grey), cream (off white), four colours, columns, rows, five colour squares in each column, five squares in each row, repeating colour patterns. Find the colour version online at https://thinkingpathwayz.weebly.com/seethinkwonder.html. As this geometric art had many components, requiring students to look for all possibilities, the students engaged in some rich discussions about what was being observed.

Prompt 2: What do you think?

Through this prompt, students were asked to push their understanding of fractions to think about how fractions were represented through this geometric art. I adapted the prompt slightly and posed the question *What fraction of the artwork do you think is represented by the colour yellow?* Students were then provided with manipulatives to work with the problem and look for ways they could apply their prior understanding of fractions to solve the problem. Through the use of manipulatives, I was able to observe which students had a strong foundational understanding of fractions, which students had some level of understanding and which students were going to require additional scaffolding, support and manipulatives to build a foundational understanding.

Prompt 3: Justify

Instead of asking students to pose wonderings, I asked them to further apply their mathematical reasoning skills to justify their thinking – the process they used to solve the problem and to finally explain their solution. As the teacher, this step allowed me to support students in developing their ability to articulate how they applied key strategies to work towards a solution to a problem. It is in this space that, as an educator, I draw great observations and formative assessment data. This helped me to see which students had a strong handle on fractions, equivalent fractions and could articulate their thought processes.

As is evident in the examples, the See Think Wonder thinking routine is very versatile and pairs nicely with the explicit teaching of problem-solving skills, building the foundation for further exploration of mathematical concepts and discussions.

Scan the QR code to find out more about the See Think Wonder thinking routine.

Connect Extend Challenge

Mathematics is full of connections between and among concepts and big ideas, and as educators it is our job to support students to experience and make those connections, in order to develop a strong mathematical understanding. The ability to connect new learning to prior learning is also an important skill students are expected to be able to do in the classroom. Building the reflective capabilities of our students to be able to identify connections, explain learning growth and flag current challenges during the learning process is something that, as educators, we need to model, support and explicitly scaffold for our learners. Just as we provide worked examples to model what success looks like, so too do we need to model as learners ourselves what connecting, extending and flagging challenges look like in a successful and reflective learner.

The thinking routine Connect Extend Challenge, developed by Ritchhart and the team at Harvard (2011), is a great routine to support this process and is another versatile routine that can be utilised in the classroom. This routine helps learners to make connections between new ideas and prior knowledge, recognise ongoing questions, puzzles and difficulties, and supports reflection on learning. This routine uses three prompts to support students:

- How are the ideas and information presented connected to what you already knew?
- What new ideas did you get that extended or broadened your thinking in new directions?
- What challenges or puzzles have come up in your mind from the ideas and information presented?

CONNECT EXTEND CHALLENGE

How are the ideas and information presented **connected** to what you already knew?

What new ideas did you get that **extended** or broadened your thinking in new directions?

What **challenges** or puzzles have come up in your mind from the ideas and information presented?

Figure 35: Connect Extend Challenge thinking routine (adapted from Ritchhart et al, 2011)

In the initial phase of development, this routine is highly structured, beginning with asking students to connect with their prior knowledge and learning, before shifting their focus to how their understanding has grown and finally recording the challenges, puzzles or wonderings they have about the concept. As this routine is used on a regular basis, both teachers and students become more comfortable with it and are able to apply it to a variety of different content areas. Moving along the phases of the development continuum means that less teacher scaffolding is required until students are able to use it seamlessly.

Adapting the routine
When I engage primary-aged students with this routine, I adapt the language in the prompt to suit the age of the learners and the context I am working in. For example, I ask:

- How did this learning connect to what you already knew?
- How did this learning extend your thinking?
- What challenged your thinking? How did you overcome this?

Prompt 1: How did this learning connect to what you already knew?
Through this prompt, students are asked to identify prior knowledge and learning experiences and find links and connections to what has been or is being learnt in the current lesson. When I engage students with this routine, I provide opportunities at the beginning of the learning experience or sequence to identify what they already know. This supports students as they learn how to make meaningful and relevant connections when reflecting learning.

When you first begin to use this routine, responses from students are often short or listed as dot points. However, the more that you as the educator model making quality connections and demonstrate how to express those words and sometimes supporting images, the better the students will become at doing this themselves.

Prompt 2: How did this learning extend your thinking?
This prompt asks students to look at their growth as a learner and how their thinking has broadened because of the learning. This is another reflective skill that requires ample modelling, scaffolding and practice. Students need to be able to look back over a learning journey, whether that be over a sequence of lessons, a term of learning or longer, and be able to identify growth. This helps learners to develop an understanding of where they need to go with their learning and work collectively to recognise how they will achieve this.

As an educator, this step in the thinking routine is an important formative assessment tool to assist me in understanding where my students are and where learning needs to go next for them. Conversations between the teacher and the student focuses on what can you, the student, do now that you couldn't do before, how you got to this point and where do we go from here. I find that this step is a nice celebration of learning achievement coupled with the alignment of new learning goals.

Prompt 3: What challenged your thinking? How did you overcome this?
Through this prompt, students are asked to articulate what their biggest sticking point or greatest challenge during the learning was. Articulating the challenge helps students to think through what made the identified area a challenge and be able to discuss that with another, whether that be a teacher, a peer or both. It is at this point that I ask students to consider:

- How they overcame their challenge, or
- What they might need to do to overcome a current challenge or sticking point

This helps students to recognise that learning is full of challenges and strategies that we apply to overcome them. It helps learners to recognise situations in the future that may be similar to which they can apply similar strategies to solve a challenge or puzzle.

Prompt 4: What do you wonder?
It is no secret that curious learners seek to understand through wonderings and investigation. When engaging students in the Connect Extend Challenge routine, both students and I inevitably end up asking questions or sharing wonderings. This is the reason I include a fourth prompt of *What do you wonder?* into the mix. This allows students to share their puzzles and engage in rich dialogue around it. Often, it is through this process that students who had identified a challenge they weren't yet about to overcome can see a solution simply through the art of posing a question and discussion with others.

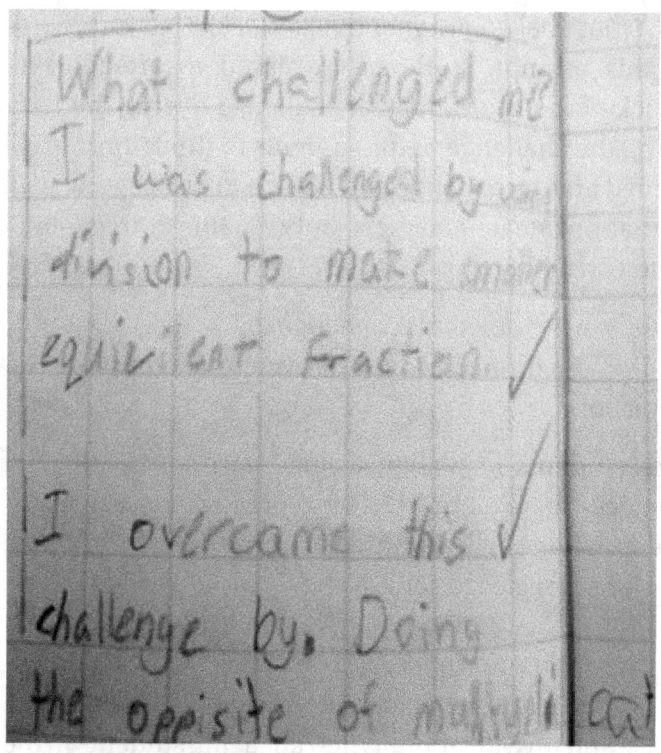

Figure 36: Connect Extend Challenge example

The more I engage students in this routine, the more reflective they become. Figure 36 highlights a small snapshot of a student's challenge and the beginning of their explanation as to how they overcame the challenge. This snapshot is an example of a student being in the initial phase of development with using this routine.

Scan the QR code to find out more about the Connect Extend Challenge thinking routine.

Chapter reflection questions

After reading chapter 7, take a moment to reflect on your learning and understanding.

1. How might you utilise these thinking routines in your classroom?
2. How do these routines help you to scaffold student thinking?
3. Choose one thinking routine to embed in your teaching and learning programme over the next month. Explicitly using it at least twice a week:
   a. Identify a range of opportunities to use the routine in Mathematics.
   b. Scaffold the students through each component of the prompts.
   c. What do you notice the first time you use the routine?
   d. What do you notice after two weeks of using the routine?
   e. What do you notice after one month of using the routine with your students?
   f. How did the thinking routine support the development of student thinking?
   g. What wonderings arose for you?
   h. What did you notice about how students articulated their thinking as they used the routine?

CHAPTER 8

Critical and creative thinking in other key learning areas

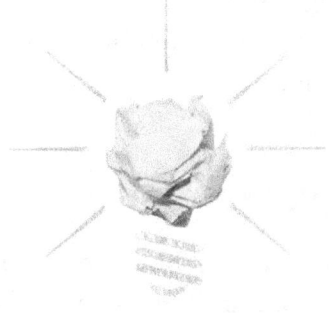

"All students can learn and think at advanced levels, and they will need practice and guidance to get there"

Richard Cash (2011)

Life is full of rich and wonderful things, and the other key learning areas taught across the curriculum in Australia help to bring those things to life in the classroom. This chapter provides a snapshot of a number of thinking routines that explore practical examples and ideas on ways teachers can embed thinking routines and other critical and creative thinking practices in other subject areas across the curriculum. It examines the purpose of specific routines, how to utilise them in the classroom and puzzles of practice from the classroom. This chapter will explore four thinking routines from the work of Ritchhart and colleagues (2011), including Think Puzzle Explore, Chalk Talk, Plus One and Layered Inference.

Chapter learning intentions

By the end of this chapter, educators will be able to:

- Identify a range of thinking routines
- Explain how thinking routines support and scaffold student thinking in other key learning areas
- Reflect on and explore the implications on their own classroom practice

Think Puzzle Explore

At the beginning of every new unit of work or sequence of learning, teachers do one very important thing – they take the time to find out what students already know about the topic or concept by activating their prior knowledge. This information helps to guide the teacher forward in the learning process. The thinking routine Think Puzzle Explore was developed by Harvard's Project Zero to help educators do exactly that (Ritchhart et al, 2011). This routine is perfect for helping students to connect to their prior knowledge, but it also takes it that next step further by inviting learners to generate ideas and develop curiosities about a topic or concept.

When I use this routine with learners, I always begin with a provocation. In its simplest form a provocation is used to provoke! They provoke thoughts, questions, interests, creativity, curiosity and ideas. They also have the potential to expand on these as well. Provocations take on a variety of forms, including images or photographs, objects and artifacts, questions, events, videos, songs, books and environments.

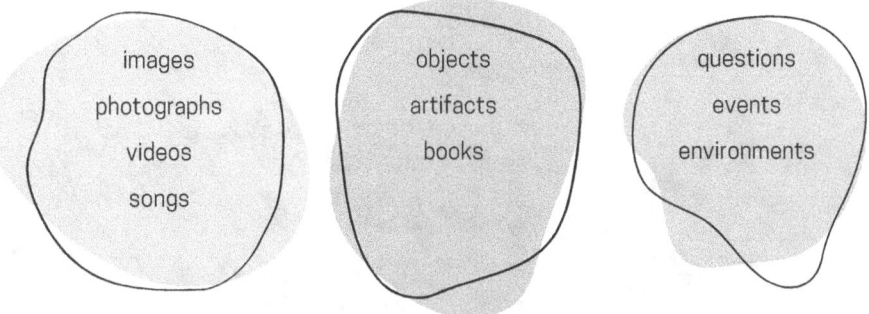

Figure 37: Types of provocations

With the stage now set for learning, I help to scaffold student thinking about the topic or concept. In the initial phases of development this is highly structured, but as the routine is used on a regular basis across all key learning areas, the students are able to use it seamlessly. This thinking routine operates using three prompts:

- What do you think you know?
- What questions or puzzles do you have?
- How might we explore the puzzles we have around this?

THINK PUZZLE EXPLORE

What do you **think** you know about this topic?

What **questions or puzzles** do you have about this topic?

How might we **explore** the puzzles we have around this topic?

Figure 38: Think Puzzle Explore thinking routine (Ritchhart et al, 2011)

Prompt 1: What do you think you know?

This prompt allows me to get a good idea of what students know and understand already about the topic or concept. It also highlights for me any misconceptions learners have or gaps in their understanding. It is important that learners are allowed to share what they think they know without any judgement or correction, as this builds a thinking culture that doesn't shame learners for not knowing yet.

When I engage students with this part of the routine, I often ask them to record their thoughts on small Post-it notes, which are then collated under the prompt *What do you think you know?* on a large piece of butcher's paper or art paper. This allows us to see our collective understanding of the topic or concept being explored and helps me, as the teacher, shape the learning moving forward.

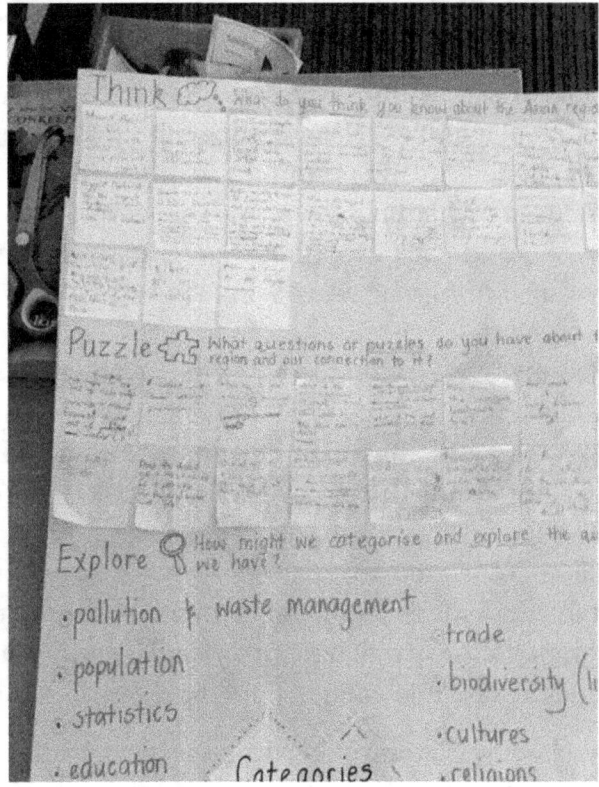

Figure 39: Think Puzzle Explore whole-class documentation example

Figure 39 highlights how I document and represent the student thinking in my classroom. This particular example is from a Year 5 and Year 6 classroom where we were exploring the unit 'A Diverse and Connected World' in Geography. This poster was put up on my classroom wall and the ongoing learning we undertake that stems from this initial thinking routine is pieced together around it.

Prompt 2: What questions or puzzles do you have?
This prompt, for me, is where the magic happens. This is where we list all of our questions, puzzles, curiosities and interests we have about the topic or concept. I find some students get really excited here when they know the answer to some of the questions, however, try to avoid letting it become a Q&A session. Combined with the Think prompt, this is what I use to drive our learning so that it is purposeful and meaningful to students.

Again, when I engage students with this prompt, I ask them to record their wonderings on small Post-it notes – one wondering per Post-it so that we can capture what we are currently curious about at the beginning of a unit or learning sequence. I glue these onto the same sheet of paper as the first prompt to capture student curiosities. These questions are what helps to shape the learning, and these are continuously referred back to so that we can show an answer to the question on our learning wall and begin to pose new wonderings.

Prompt 3: How might we explore the puzzles we have around this?
I think students find this prompt the most challenging. I have experimented with different ways to approach and scaffold this prompt until I found something that worked for both the students and I in terms of what we were wanting to get out of this prompt, other than your stock standard response of *Just google it*. The way that I scaffold this prompt for students is laying out all of the Post-it notes from the previous prompt (before we glue them on) and identify questions that would fit under a particular category or follow a certain theme.

We begin to collectively group and categorise the questions, providing explanations for why one question is being paired with another. Once each of the questions is sorted, you begin to see some key areas emerging in the wonderings. It is through these categories that our learning journey forward can be 'chunked' into smaller components to help us better understand the topic and concepts we are exploring and address the things we are wondering through engaging with the syllabus content. From here, we record the key categories on the large paper so that they can be easily identifiable.

This routine provides educators with an easy tool to bring student voice into the learning environment through their wonderings and curiosities. It is through utilising this routine as a driver of future learning that students can see the true impact of the questions and wonderings they have in shaping their learning journey. This is important for students to experience in their schooling journeys so that they can build and refine this skill and apply it as a lifelong learner long after they leave the walls of the classroom.

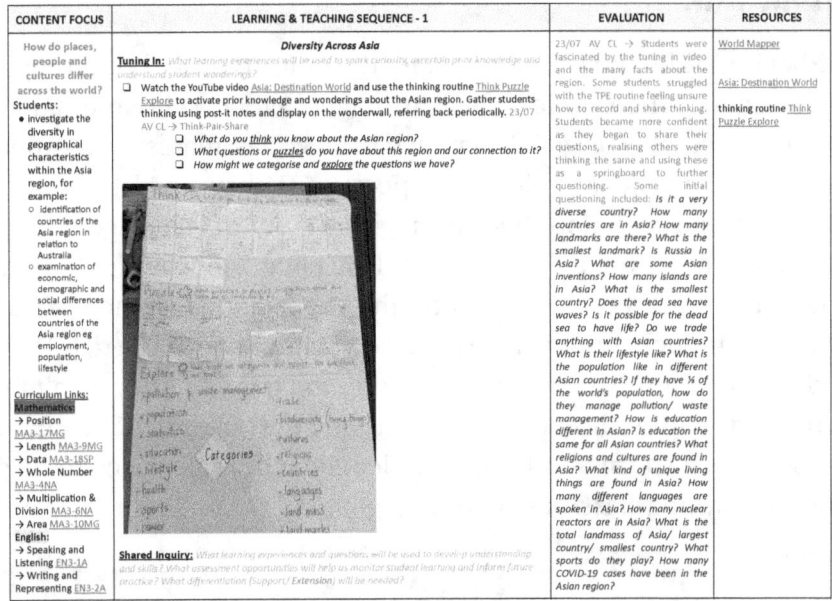

Figure 40: Programming and evaluation Think Puzzle Explore example

As an educator, it is important that we capture this rich learning in our programming and evaluation. Figure 40 highlights a small example of how I capture the thinking, wonderings and learning of the students in my classroom. In my teaching and learning programme, I include photographic evidence of whole-class or snapshots of small-group or individual student responses during the thinking routine as a learning artifact. I add this straight into the appropriate part of the programme and record any observations I noticed and the wonderings that were posed during the learning. As the teacher, this helps me to monitor the learning over time and ensure that future learning is responsive to the needs of the students.

Scan the QR code to find out more about the Think Puzzle Explore thinking routine.

The Thinking Classroom   7

Chalk Talk

The beginning of a new school year is an exciting time for both students and teachers. When students walk through their new classroom doors in weeks to come, they will be greeted by new classmates, a new room, a new teacher and a variety of expectations they need to know in order to be successful in this learning space. A few years ago, I began thinking about why, as the teacher, I dictated the way the learning environment looked, operated and the expectations we had of each other. This thought inspired me to make a change and take a risk. When students walk through my classroom door on day one, they won't find a Pinterest-worthy classroom. What they do find are individual names on the door, a warm and friendly welcome and a safe space to begin building a strong classroom culture together.

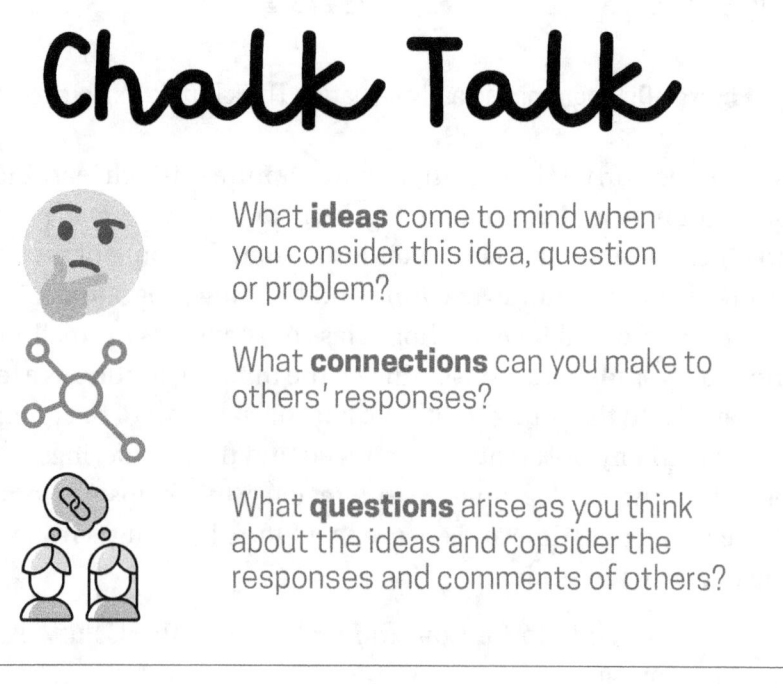

Figure 41: Chalk Talk thinking routine (Ritchhart et al, 2011)

One of the experiences we engage in is a Chalk Talk thinking routine (Ritchhart et al, 2011). This routine is perfect for helping students to consider questions, problems and ideas through sharing their thoughts, opinions and wonderings about the prompt and responding to the thoughts of others. Through this routine, we explore our expectations around the learning environment and the way we interact within in it. On separate sheets of paper, I pose the following questions:

- What does a quality learning environment look like?
- What does a quality learning environment sound like?
- What does a quality learning environment feel like?
- What do you think you need from the teacher to be a successful learner this year?
- How might you extend and apply your learning beyond the classroom?
- What interests you? What are you passionate about?

As students walk around the room examining the prompts with their small group, they record their own thoughts to each of the prompts, examine the thinking of others, elaborate on the thinking of others by adding further information and find connections between ideas before being directed to shift to the next prompt. After students have recorded their thinking on each prompt, they gather in small groups to re-examine one of the prompts. When re-examining, they look for key ideas that are represented multiple times and they look for ideas that connect in a meaningful way to other ideas, building a stronger idea about our expectations.

As a class, we come together to share what we discovered about the key ideas and explain why we think they are important for our learning environment this year. This list of key ideas the students have revised and developed form the basis for our classroom expectations and learning behaviours that we agree are important for our class to be successful this year, including myself as the teacher. These key ideas are displayed within the classroom and are routinely revisited and revised based on our current needs as a class. For example, we look at what is working well for us as a group, what areas we are not yet achieving and need further developing, and what goals will help us to get there.

Figure 42: Chalk Talk whole-class behaviour expectations example

At the beginning of every term, we spend time looking back over our key ideas looking for ways we can make adjustments and improvements to our expectations, continually striving to do better and be better as a group. As the teacher, this is the most important learning experience we undertake. **Why?** It is important because it signals to students that this space we share together is not just my space, but is theirs, too. It is a space that values their ideas, their opinions, their input, their understanding and their respect. It is also an experience that allows me to find out what students are passionate about, what makes them tick, how they interact with and share ideas with others, and what they hope to achieve in this learning environment and how they think I can help them get there.

Scan the QR code to find out more about the Chalk Talk thinking routine.

Plus One

How often do you ask students to read, listen or watch something and ask them to record down key pieces of information? It might be after listening to a guest speaker or after watching a video clip in science or the humanities that you ask students to record down all the key details they can remember about the topic. For many of our students, the thought of doing this overwhelms them as they struggle to recall copious amounts of information. This is one of the reasons why I utilise the thinking routine Plus One in my classroom. Developed by Ritchhart and Church (2020), this routine helps learners to identify ideas from a stimulus and make additions, elaborations and connections to the thinking of others. It is a great alternative to the traditional note-taking exercise. This routine follows a number of steps to support students:

- **Recall** – after viewing the stimulus, students take three minutes to record as many key points and important details that they can remember independently.
- **Pass right and add one** – students pass their page/scaffold to the person on their right and add, elaborate or connect. Students are asked to add *one* new idea that is missing, or elaborate on an existing idea by adding further detail or show the connection between ideas on their partner's page.
- **Repeat** – pass the page again and repeat the *pass right and add one* step at least two times.
- **Review** – students examine their original page, reading through and reviewing any additions, elaborations and connections. Students add any additional ideas they gained from reading the work of others.

- **Reflect** – students reflect on the process of using the routine to gather and record information by reflecting on the following questioning prompts:
    - What did you find as you read the ideas of others?
    - How did this routine help you as a learner?
    - How did it help you build on the thinking of others?
    - How did it help you to build your understanding of what you just viewed?
    - What worked well and what did you find challenging?
    - How does this routine push your thinking?
    - How might we make this work for us?

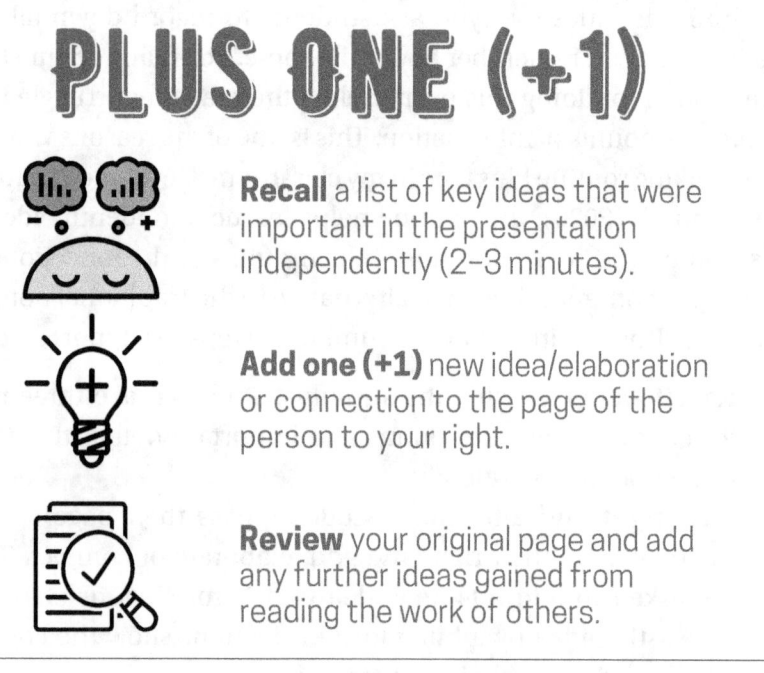

Figure 43: Plus One thinking routine (Ritchhart et al, 2020)

This routine is a regular feature in my classroom, especially when working in the curriculum areas of Science, History and Geography, as students in the primary grades learn to take notes and capture information. While the act of note taking or reading over one's notes is generally not considered an effective strategy, the use of the Plus One routine helps to facilitate effective filtering of information, increases in-class participation while engaging with ideas and promotes the construction of memories (Ritchhart & Church, 2020).

The stimulus

The type of stimulus I use in combination with the Plus One thinking routine can vary. But it is important to note that whatever stimulus you use, students require multiple exposures to it in order to understand and gain the information they need for the stimulus. In my classroom, I present the stimulus to the students asking them to read, listen or watch. After they have examined the stimulus, I engage the students in a discussion about the stimulus using questioning prompts before re-examining the stimulus with the intent of capturing key ideas afterwards. Depending on the stimulus, this might happen over one lesson or span multiple lessons.

Recall

The purpose of this prompt is for students to recall as many key points and important details as they can. Students will do this to varying degrees of success, which is why I really like the remaining steps in this routine to support students in gathering key information and details. I provide my students with a template to record their information in dot points and track the steps we have completed, especially in the initial phases of using this routine (see figure 44). Providing students with a time indication is an important part of helping them understand the value of the task and how long they have to undertake the recall of information.

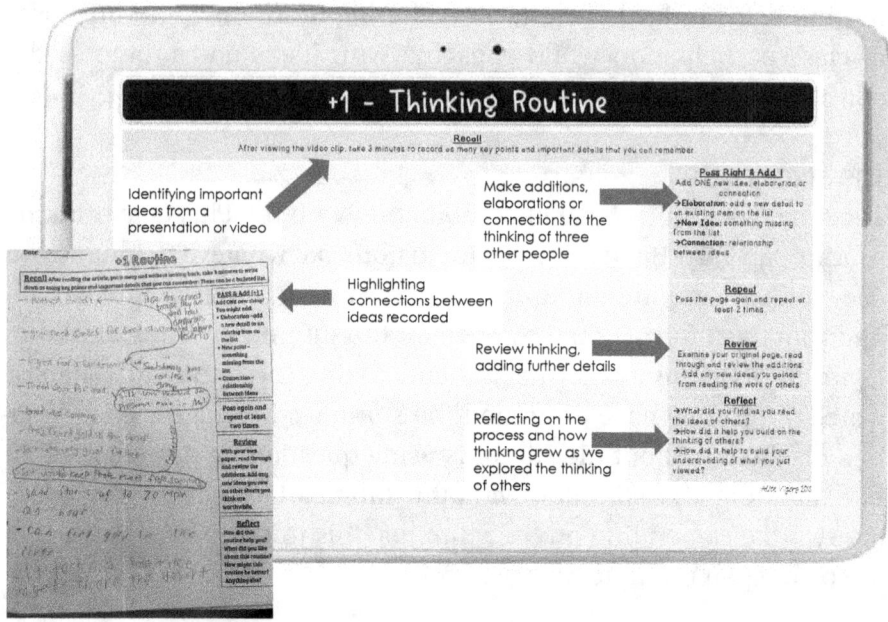

Figure 44: Plus One thinking routine example

Pass right and add one

This is where the magic begins to happen. By passing their page or scaffold to the right, students are able to read through the information gathered by others and do one or more things with this information. Firstly, students are asked to look at how they might add new information and key ideas to what the person has already added on their page. This addition provides the original owner of the page with further information they will be able to draw upon further in the learning journey. Secondly, students are asked to add any elaborations to the page through recording additional details to an existing idea on the list. This supports learners as they learn to provide clarity around ideas and commit key details to memory. Finally, students are asked to make connections between ideas listed on the page, helping the original owner of the page to see the relationship between and among key pieces of information about a topic or stimulus. This step is undertaken at least twice so that two other students have collaborated on each student's page.

Review

It is through this prompt that I support my students to examine their original piece of paper or template by reading what has been added and adding anything further they gathered from reading other people's brainstorm of key ideas. As I have engaged students with this routine, I have found that rarely do we get to this phase without every student having something to add from the work of another. The students who began with only a small amount on their original page all of a sudden feel more confident to use and discuss this information in the next phase of learning.

Reflect

One of the greatest things about using thinking routines in the classroom to scaffold critical and creative thinking and support the development of content knowledge is the ability to build in reflection on thinking and learning. It is through the questioning prompts in this phase that I guide students through the identification of key ideas and important details, and explore how the routine supported us to build this understanding. We also examine how we can use this information and the skills we are building to further develop our learning in the coming lessons, connecting where we have come to where we are going.

Scan the QR code to find out more about the Plus One thinking routine.

Layered Inference

The ability to make inferences is a skill students find challenging and is therefore something they require explicit instruction and modelled scaffolding in, in order to develop this complex skill over time. There is not a single subject area in the curriculum that does not require the use of inferencing at one point or another. The Layered Inference thinking routine (Roberts, 2013) is a tool that teachers can employ across a variety of subject areas to support students to develop higher-order thinking skills through the process of developing inference around a given stimulus. It is through the scaffolding of this routine that teachers are able to support students in distinguishing between what is explicitly provided to them in a given stimulus and what is missing. There are a number of key prompts that guide the layering of meaning in this routine:

- What does this source tell me?
- What can I infer from the source? What guesses can I make?
- What does the source not tell me?
- What else would I like to find out? What other questions do I need to ask? Where might I get the information?

LAYERED INFERENCE

1. What does this source tell me?

2. What can I infer from the source? What guesses can I make?

3. What does the source not tell me?

4. What else would I like to find out? What other questions do I need to ask? Where might I get the information?

Figure 45: Layered Inference thinking routine (Roberts, 2013)

In my classroom, I often engage students in this routine when examining an artwork, photograph or artifact in History, Geography or Creative Arts, although it can be used quite effectively in other key learning areas, such as in literacy or numeracy. What teachers need to carefully consider is why they want students to unpack this stimulus at a deeper level and what they want students to do with that information moving forward.

The stimulus

This thinking routine uses a core stimulus to support students to dig deeper into ideas. The type of stimulus that teachers can draw upon to do this is wide ranging, including images, photographs, artifacts, graphs, diagrams, data tables and primary or secondary sources. Students should be provided with time to examine the stimulus and any available contextual information, such as a caption.

Prompt 1: What does this source tell me?
Through this prompt, I ask students to record what is directly stated in the stimulus. For example, in figure 46, I asked students to examine an artwork depicting life on the Australian gold fields, and list down all the things they could see. By doing this, students were able to record the facts, identifying the directly stated information from the artwork, such as a small creek, different equipment for gold panning, trees and a few tents along the creek.

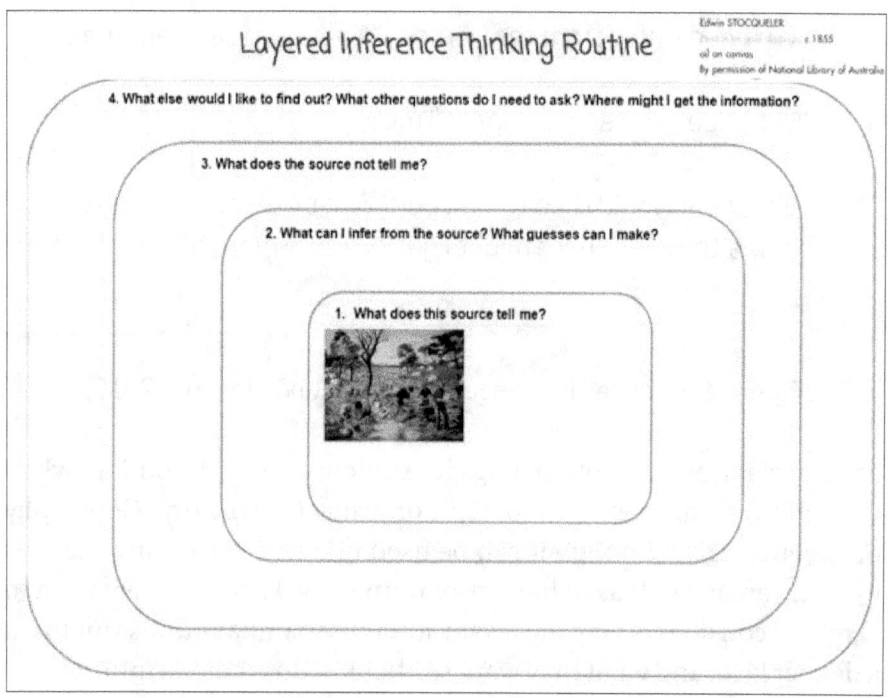

Figure 46: Layered Inference thinking routine example

Prompt 2: What can I infer from the source? What guesses can I make?
Through this prompt, I support students to think about inferences we can make about the stimulus. This requires students to draw upon their knowledge of concepts and ideas that directly relate to their content knowledge and observations about what is directly stated in the stimulus. This is a more complex skill than what is being asked of students in prompt 1 and requires the teacher to model, use think alouds and scaffold students' thinking as they learn to make informed

inferences. For example, the gold fields artwork only shows men panning for gold. This observation led to inferences about where the women and children might be and what they might be doing based on students' historical knowledge of the 1850s and life on the gold fields.

Prompt 3: What does the source not tell me?
This prompt asks students to consider ideas and information that is not available in the stimulus, but is related and relevant to it. This requires students to think about what other information might be useful in understanding the stimulus. For example, the gold fields artwork does not explicitly indicate the exact location of the gold fields being depicted, the time of year, how people travelled there, how long they spent there, etc.

Prompt 4: What else would I like to find out? What other questions do I need to ask? Where might I get the information?
This prompt asks students to consider the questions, wonderings and curiosities that arose from examining and discussing the stimulus. It is through the fourth layer that students extend their thinking beyond the stimulus by considering what needs to be explored next. As a teacher, this step in the thinking routine gives great insight into what students are wondering in relation to the stimulus. It is through observing these wonderings that teachers can draw upon these to drive student learning and inquiry to discover further information and dig deeper into the content.

Scan the QR code to find out more about the Layered Inference thinking routine.

Chapter reflection questions

After reading chapter 8, take a moment to reflect on your learning and understanding.

1. How might you utilise these thinking routines in your classroom?
2. How do these routines help you to scaffold student thinking?
3. Choose one thinking routine to embed in your teaching and learning programme over the next month. Explicitly using it at least twice a week:
   a. Identify a range of opportunities to use the routine in a curriculum area.
   b. Scaffold the students through each component of the prompts.
   c. What do you notice the first time you use the routine?
   d. What do you notice after two weeks of using the routine?
   e. What do you notice after one month of using the routine with your students?
   f. How did the thinking routine support the development of student thinking?
   g. What wonderings arose for you?
   h. What did you notice about how students articulated their thinking as they used the routine?

CHAPTER 9

Feedback and self-reflection

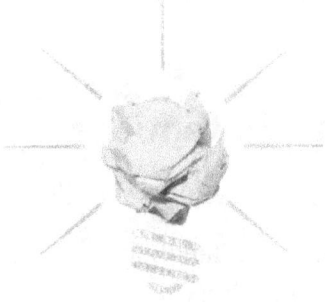

*"We don't learn from experiences;
we learn from reflecting on the experience"*

John Dewey

While most people engage in reflection on a daily basis, much of this occurs in quiet moments by ourselves. Most students are not used to reflecting on their learning in a structured manner. They will need some help to develop skills in reflective thinking and writing. While this skill may be new to them at first, they will become more familiar with it as they progress. The Australian curriculum and other state syllabus documents highlight the importance of developing our students' ability to be self-reflective and to give and receive feedback through *Assessment As Learning* practices. Thinking routines are a great way to help students and teachers name, notice and develop their thinking dispositions.

This chapter explores ways teachers can embed self-reflection and feedback practices into the classroom while supporting the development of students' critical and creative thinking skills and metacognitive processes. It examines the purpose of specific routines, how to utilise them in the classroom and puzzles of practice from the classroom. This chapter will explore four reflection routines, including 4-Square Criterion Reflection, 3, 2, 1 Reflection, Traffic Light Reflection and Give 3.

Chapter learning intentions

By the end of this chapter, educators will be able to:

- Understand the role of feedback and self-reflection in the development of thinking
- Explain how reflective thinking routines support and scaffold a student's ability to think about and reflect upon their thinking
- Reflect on and explore the implications on their own classroom practice

Self-reflection

When we ask students to reflect, how many of them would actually know what that means? How many students in our classrooms know what effective reflection looks like?

Self-reflection is the evaluation or judgement of one's performance and the identification of one's strengths and weaknesses with a view to improving one's learning outcomes (Demore, 2017). In a classroom setting, reflecting 'in' and 'on' learning helps our learners to:

- Become more aware of the knowledge and skills they have developed
- Identify strengths and areas for development
- Develop future learning goals
- Gain greater understanding of themselves and how they learn
- Take more responsibility for their learning
  (National Council for Curriculum and Assessment, 2015)

Just like we do when we use thinking routines as strategic vehicles in which to scaffold the thinking of our learners, self-reflective practices of both teachers and students move through different developmental phases. These include from initial introduction of a self-reflective strategy to the development of it as a strategic tool to reflect on learning through to the advanced integration of reflective strategies to evaluate and promote their own learning and growth.

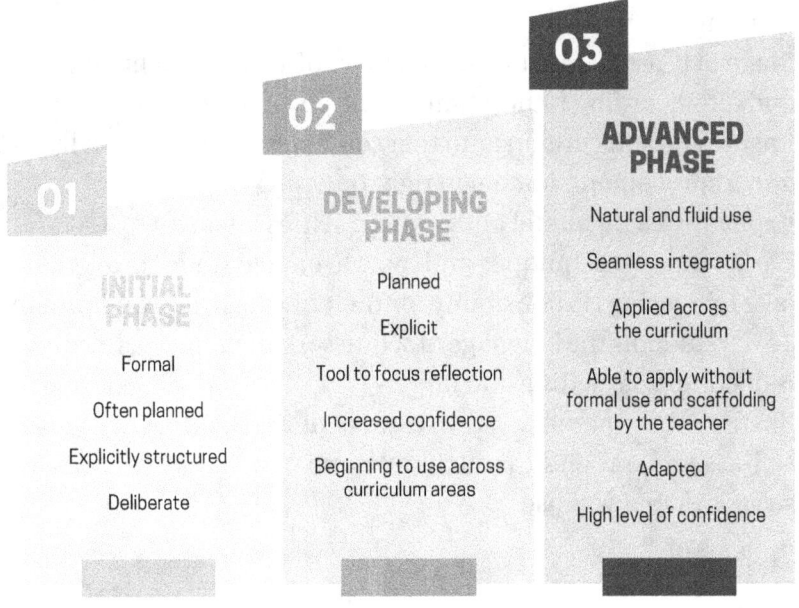

Figure 47: Phases of reflective thinking development (Vigors, 2019)

When I first introduce reflective strategies and tools to students, they are formal, deliberate and planned. I explicitly structure them to help scaffold reflection and use think alouds to model my own reflection using the tool or strategy. I repeatedly use them across the curriculum to help build student confidence and competence to move from the initial phase towards using the reflective strategies as a tool and beyond to their seamless and natural use in a variety of situations.

When introducing self-assessment:

- Provide guided opportunities to self-assess
- Provide students with feedback on the 'quality' of their self-assessments
- Teach students how to use feedback from self-assessments to set learning goals and plan the next steps
- Demonstrate how students can monitor their learning and progress towards their goals

To support self-assessment:

- Provide opportunities for students to self-assess at all stages of the learning process
- Make self-assessment a regular part of what students do during and after learning rather than a 'bolt-on' activity
- Ensure students understand that self-assessment is about learning and improvement, not being right or wrong
- Explicitly teach, model and scaffold self-assessment
- Use a range of techniques and tools to enable students to gradually take increasing responsibility for their own learning and progress
- Teach students the language of self-assessment, such as evaluation, reflection, goal setting and targets
- Ensure that parents and carers understand why you use self-assessment and that it is only one of a variety of assessment strategies that you use

4-Square Criterion Reflection

Utilising the success criteria as part of the self-reflective and evaluative process is a crucial component of helping students recognise growth in their thinking and learning, and identify ways to move learning forward in order to achieve the success criteria for the lesson or leaning sequence. The 4-Square Criterion Reflection (adapted from Carroll, 2018) is a great way for students to self-assess themselves against the success criteria for the lesson. In my classroom we focus on no more than four criteria for success in any lesson, with each box representing an area we are focusing our attention on in the learning artifact. This reflective routine has a number of key components, such as:

- Four success criteria (maximum) identified for the lesson focus and explicit instruction; these are made visible in the classroom and written alongside the students' learning artifact so that they can be referred back to over time.
- Four boxes are drawn near the success criteria; one box for each criterion focus area.
- Self-assessment and peer assessment against the criterion recorded in the appropriate box.
- Use the reflection of achievement as a way to develop and record individualised learning goals for future lessons.

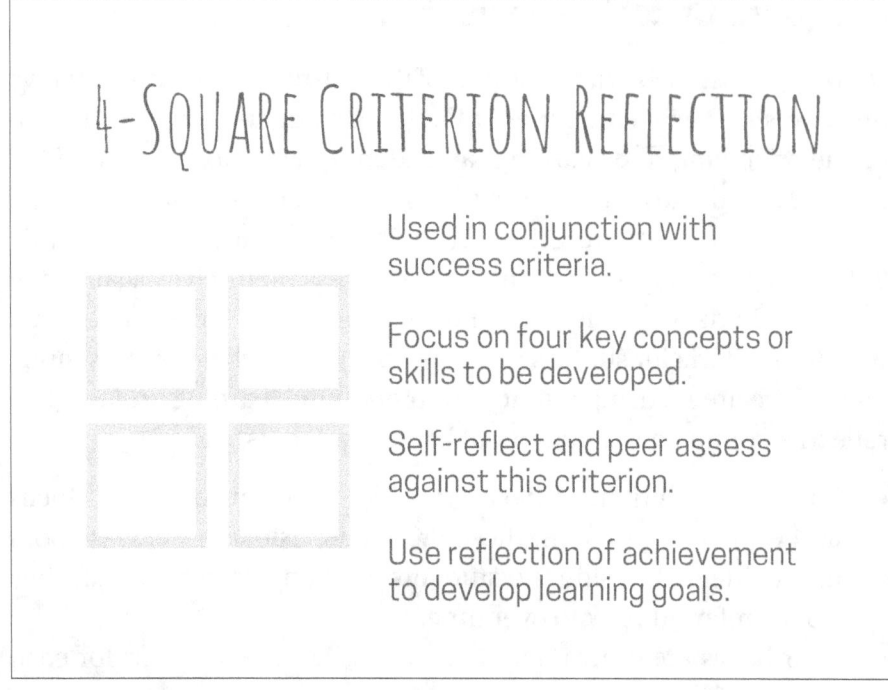

Figure 48: 4-Square Criterion Reflection thinking routine (adapted from Carroll, 2018)

When I engage students in writing lessons, I use a maximum of four success criteria that will be the focus elements of review and feedback for this piece of writing. I have found that this practice helps reduce the cognitive load for students, as it decreases the number of things to focus on in their writing and helps them to continuously build solid writing strategies in a 'chunked' way.

Along with the lesson's learning intention, I have students record the success criteria in their books as a way to refer back to what they needed to be successful in this piece of writing. I combine this focus on four success criteria with a practice I call 4-Square Criterion Reflection, which I use as a student self-assessment, goal-setting, peer assessment and teacher-to-student feedback tool. Each of the four boxes represents one of the elements of the success criteria.

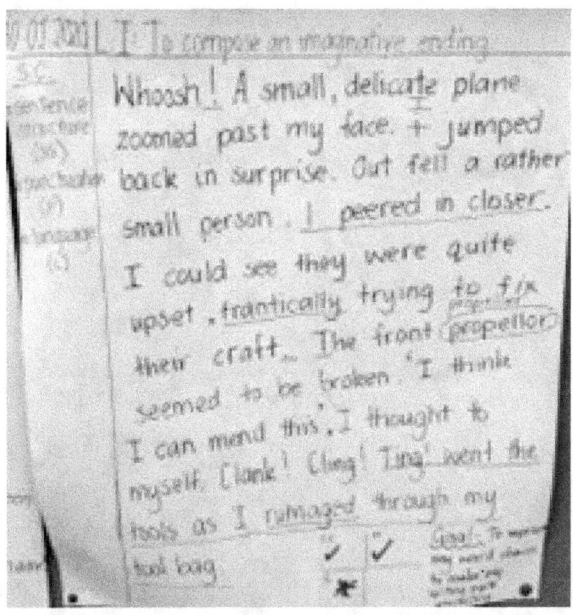

Figure 49: 4-Square Criterion Reflection modelled example

When students self-assess their writing, I have them re-read through their work four times, each time focusing on a different element of the success criteria and finding examples to support the achievement of that success criteria. I have them tick the box if they feel they have achieved that criterion and put a star if they feel it is still an area they need to work on. From here I have them identify one area they would like to further develop in the next writing session. Undertaking practice in this way helps students to see the value in proofreading, editing and re-crafting, and supports the development of specific and measurable goals for learning.

This also helps us as teachers to target our feedback to specific areas of writing, rather than the process as a whole. It also reduces the amount of marking we as teachers have to do, as the areas of focus are limited to four elements, giving us more time to conference with students about where they are and where to next bring formative assessment to life.

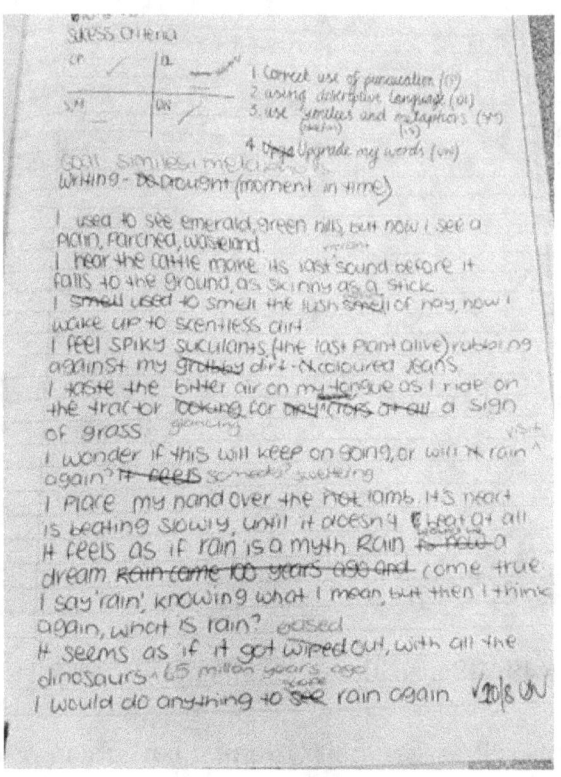

Figure 50: 4-Square Criterion Reflection student example

This reflective practice routine is not confined to the writing lesson and is in fact versatile and adaptable to all curriculum areas. Engaging students in self and peer reflection as well as using the reflective routine to drive feedback in the classroom is an essential part of building a learning culture that values feedback, is constructive with suggested improvements and celebrates the learning successes no matter how small.

Scan the QR code to find out more about the 4-Square Criterion Reflection thinking routine.

3, 2, 1 Reflection

Reflecting back on our thinking and growth as a learner is an important skill for all students to develop. It can sometimes feel like a daunting task for educators to build this into their practice but is something that is hugely beneficial for both teacher and student, and once routinely undertaken in the classroom, becomes part of the fabric of how things are 'done' in that learning space. The 3, 2, 1 Reflection thinking routine is an adaption of the well-known routine 3, 2, 1 Bridge developed by Ritchhart, Church and Morrison in 2011, and is a useful scaffold to support students as they become self-regulated learners. This routine asks learners to think about:

- What they know now as a result of the learning
- Any questions or puzzles they still have about the area of study
- What still challenges them about the learning that they feel they haven't grasped yet

The 3, 2, 1 Bridge thinking routine was something that I used regularly in my classroom and saw the value in identifying initial thinking and wonderings and connecting those to new learning. From that I began to adapt the routine to form part of our self-reflective practices on learning. This reflective thinking routine has three components that support students to think about the learning they have engaged with, such as:

- Record three things that have been learnt
- List two questions that are still lingering about the learning
- Identify one challenge that was faced during the learning experience

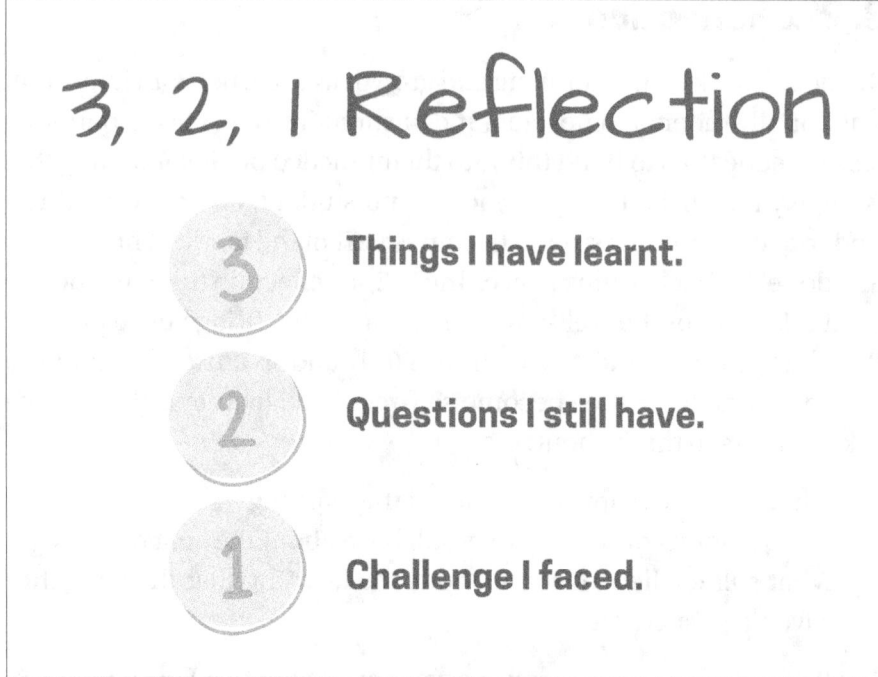

Figure 51: 3, 2, 1 Reflection thinking routine
(adapted from Ritchhart et al, 2011)

Prompt 1: 3 things I have learnt
Through this prompt, I support students to recall and record three new things they have learnt through engaging with the learning experience. This helps learners to see that learning, no matter how small, is still important in helping us to grow and develop, and achieve our learning goals in the classroom.

Prompt 2: 2 questions I still have
Through this prompt, I ask students to think about two things they are still wondering or are curious about that wasn't addressed or fully covered in the learning experience. As an educator this helps me to see what students are connecting to the learning experience, any misconceptions that might still be lingering and how to use these questions to support the next phase of learning development.

Prompt 3: 1 challenge I faced

Through this prompt, I support students to recognise learning challenges (big and small) that they faced during the learning experience and engage in reflective discussions with students about how they overcame these. This supports students as they learn to employ a range of strategies to overcome problems and apply these skills when faced with the same or a similar challenge into the future.

Scan the QR code to find out more about the 3, 2, 1 Reflection thinking routine.

Traffic Light Reflection

One of the easiest ways to begin supporting students to reflect on their learning, not only at the end of learning but throughout the learning process, is to utilise a colour-coding system. The Traffic Light Reflection routine is an adaptation of Ritchhart, Church and Morrison's Red Light, Yellow Light thinking routine (2011). This reflective thinking routine invites learners to examine their current understanding of concepts and skills through:

- Utilising a colour-coding system
- Examining where learning is currently at
- Identifying ways learning could move forward
- Justifying their response with reasoning

The use of the visual coding system helps learners to recognise different phases in the learning process that support us as we move from not knowing to knowing, and the connection to our prior knowledge.

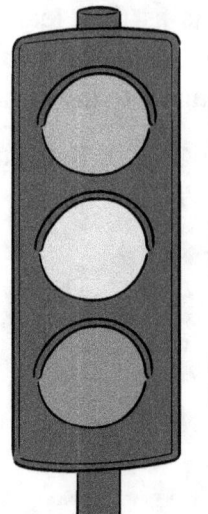

Figure 52: Traffic Light Reflection thinking routine (adapted from Ritchhart et al, 2011)

Setting up the routine

In my classroom, I display the routine visually so that students understand what the different colour prompts represent when we are self-reflecting on our learning. I don't deviate from these representations so that over time students can identify the representations without the visual prompt. I ask learners to pause and think about the learning they are currently engaged with or have just undertaken, and ask them to think about which colour representation fits with how they currently feel they are travelling in their learning journey.

Choosing a colour

Through this phase, I ask students to record a coloured circling in the margin of their page to visually represent where they feel they are at with their learning. This is a great observational snapshot and feedback for me as the teacher to pinpoint the students who feel they require more support and further scaffolding. When I conference with students who choose the yellow or red colour code, I add a dot point or two to identify what the focused support will be. This helps me to monitor and keep track of the on-the-go differentiations I make for students to support their learning and longitudinally identify any trends emerging.

Scan the QR code to find out more about the Traffic Light Reflection thinking routine.

Feedback

Giving students feedback in the classroom during the learning process has been proven to increase learning and improve student outcomes. When given correctly, feedback guides the student in their learning process and gives them the direction they need to reach the target or goal of the lesson. Effective feedback is focused on performance and solely concerned with helping students' close gaps in their knowledge. Effective feedback:

- Recognises and reinforces success and high-quality work
- Gives specific suggestions about how to modify and improve work that does not meet the success criteria for a constructed response

The main purpose of feedback is to reduce discrepancies between a learning intention and current understanding, behaviours and performance. Feedback is effective when students:

- Can monitor the quality of their work as they produce it
- Know what high-quality work is and how their work compares

(Hopkins & Craig, 2015)

NESA highlights that teacher feedback about student learning is essential for students and integral to teaching, learning and assessment (NSW Education Standards Authority, n.d.). Feedback can clarify for students:

- How their knowledge, understanding and skills are developing in relation to the syllabus outcomes and content being addressed
- How to improve their learning

NESA further explains the principles of effective feedback: Feedback enables students to recognise their strengths as well as areas for development, and to identify and plan with their teacher the next steps in their learning. Students should be provided with opportunities to improve their knowledge, understanding and skills through feedback that:

- Is timely, specific and related to the learning and assessment intention
- Is constructive and provides meaningful information to students about their learning in a variety of forms
- Focuses on the activity and corrects misunderstandings
- Identifies and reinforces students' strengths
- Provides information about how they can improve
- Facilitates the development of and provides opportunities for self-assessment and reflection during the learning process
- Informs future teaching and learning opportunities

Give 3

The art of giving and receiving feedback is something that is often reserved for the teacher in many classrooms, however, with a strong emphasis on *Assessment As Learning* practices in the Australian curriculum, educators are required to support students to develop their feedback capabilities alongside being a self-reflective learner. The Give 3 feedback routine invites learners to examine the work of others with the aim of identifying positives and improves. It also provides an opportunity for peers to seek clarification in order to support learning growth. This feedback routine came out of a need I saw in my classroom back in 2017, as I worked with my students to build and embed feedback structures into the classroom. This routine consists of three phases:

- Identify one positive from the piece of work
- Highlight one thing that needs further clarification or explaining
- Provide one suggestion for improvement

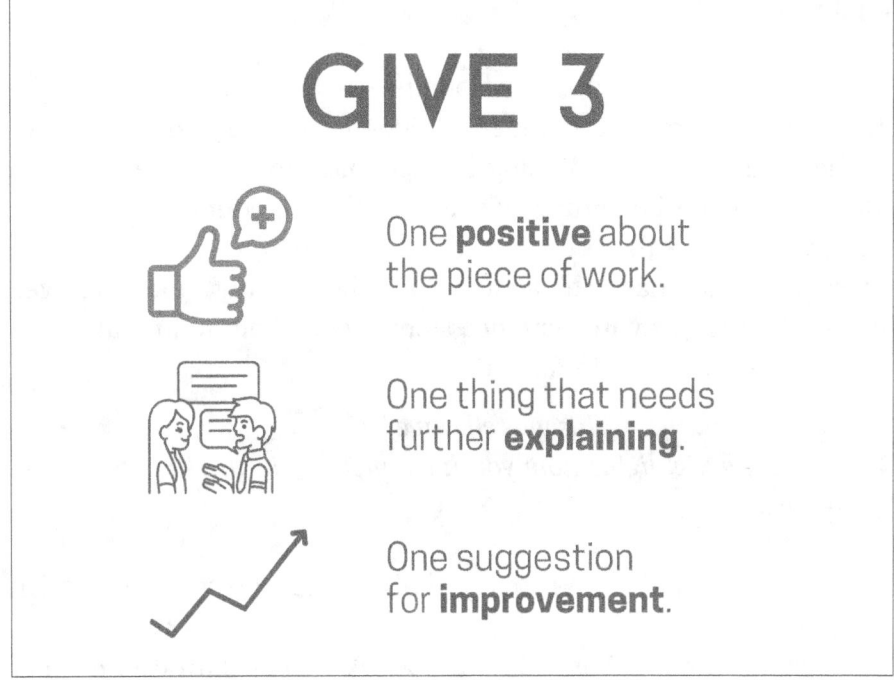

Figure 53: Give 3 feedback thinking routine (Vigors, 2019)

When I utilise this feedback routine in the classroom with my students, I model, scaffold and structure student feedback using sentence stems. These sentence stems help to focus student thinking, observations and feedback to a peer resulting in more meaningful and constructive feedback beyond 'It was good'.

Launching the routine
This routine works perfectly in a paired situation. Utilising grouping structures you already have in place in the classroom, group your students in pairs, providing each student with their partner's work. If the work sample is a piece of writing, I ask the 'author' of the text to read the piece of work to their feedback partner while they follow along. It is important to note that peer-to-peer feedback requires a

great deal of scaffolding and modelling by the teacher before students are asked to undertake peer-to peer-feedback on their own. This is crucial to ensure the integrity of peer-to-peer feedback and to help students to see and understand the role that peer-to-peer feedback has on their learning.

Prompt 1: Identify one positive from the piece of work

Through this prompt, I ask students to identify the strengths or positives in their partner's work, linking this feedback to the success criteria identified at the beginning of the learning experience. Supporting students to make these connections helps them to observe when a success criterion has been achieved or when it's not quite there yet. Providing students with sentence stems helps them to articulate the positives of a learning artifact, such as:

- *I noticed that ___ . This was effective because ___ .*
- *___ really highlights how you have met ___ in the success criteria because ___ .*

Prompt 2: Highlight one thing that needs further clarification or explaining

Through this prompt, I ask students to seek further clarification about one aspect of the learning artifact that they are unsure about. This is where we scaffold wonderings to seek additional information. This phase is important as it helps the 'author' or 'creator' of the work learn to provide clarity around what they create. Again, I use sentence stems to support students through this phase, such as:

- *What did you mean by ___ ?*
- *Tell me more about ___ .*
- *Can you tell me why ___ ?*

Prompt 3: Provide one suggestion for improvement

This prompt is where students are scaffolded to identify an area for improvement in their partner's learning artifact, linked to the success criteria for the learning sequence. Supporting students to identify an area for growth and be able to articulate that to a peer takes modelling, scaffolding and lots of training, as students learn to not only notice but to communicate constructive feedback that is conducive to moving learning forward.

Scan the QR code to find out more about the Give 3 feedback thinking routine.

Chapter reflection questions

After reading chapter 9, take a moment to reflect on your learning and understanding.

1. How might you utilise these thinking routines in your classroom?
2. What role does self-reflection and feedback play in your classroom?
3. How do you purposefully plan time for self-reflection at different phases of learning?
4. How do you intentionally model your own self-reflections using think alouds so that your thought processes are shared and made visible?
5. How do you use the language of self-reflection in order to provide students with the vocabulary to be able to describe and reflect on their own learning?
6. How do you consider how the environment supports and fosters self-reflection on learning (static vs interactive displays, layout)?
7. How do you engage in thoughtful conversations and learning conferences with students about their learning?
8. How do you utilise scaffolds and prompts to support the development of self-reflection capabilities in your learners?
9. How do you focus on the value of constructive and critical reflections that help to drive learning forward?
10. How do you strategically plan and provide opportunities for students to engage in self-reflection and peer reflection as part of their ongoing experience in the classroom?

PART FOUR
ASSESSING STUDENT THINKING

CHAPTER 10

How do we assess students' thinking?

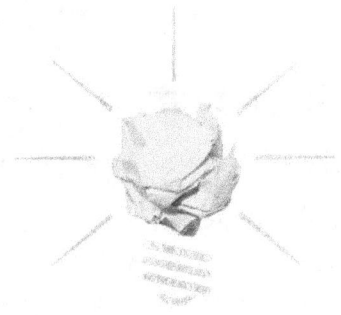

"The world as we have created it is a process of our thinking. It cannot be changed without changing our thinking"

Albert Einstein

How do you measure thinking?

This question, posed by Ron Ritchhart in 2018 at a Cultures of Thinking workshop for leaders, made me stop and think about my own students. How do I measure their thinking? And how do I utilise this knowledge to push their thinking further? Measuring student thinking has the potential to be a tricky endeavour. It requires teachers to strategically plan for and implement strategies that allow students ample opportunities to share and demonstrate their level of thinking across a broad range of subject areas (Vigors, 2018).

This chapter explores how teachers can leverage formal and informal assessment experiences to build an understanding of how a student's thinking is developing over time, the development of a shared language and how metacognitive processes link to the learning processes. It highlights how *Assessment For* and *As Learning* experiences provide powerful opportunities for students to share their thinking with teachers and their peers, alongside ways to leverage thinking routines as assessment vehicles.

> **Chapter learning intentions**
>
> By the end of this chapter, educators will be able to:
>
> - Understand the role of assessment in the development of student thinking
> - Identify ways we can leverage thinking routines as part of the assessment process

In *Clarity*, researcher and educator Lyn Sharratt (2019) highlights:

> *"Nothing else matters in teaching and learning as much as quality assessment, that is, data that inform and differentiate instruction for each learner in a never-ending cycle of inquiry to discover what works best"*

As an educator, this sits at the core of what we do. The role of assessment in classrooms should be used to inform and drive the teaching and learning process in an ongoing manner. Assessment can take many forms, but it is through the integration of a range of assessment types into the teaching and learning process that has the greatest impact. In this chapter we refer to three types of assessment:

1. *Assessment For Learning*
2. *Assessment As Learning*
3. *Assessment Of Learning*

The term 'assessment' is derived from the Latin word *assidere*, meaning 'to sit beside'. This idea of sitting beside to ascertain where a student is at and gain a clear vision of what is possible and how to move learning forward is a beautiful one. It alludes to the notion of a continuous cycle or process of knowledge and skill development, and the ongoing pursuit of meaning making in order to develop a greater understanding of concepts (Sharratt, 2019). In the classroom, it is one thing to support students to be critical and creative thinkers, and it is another to be able to identify growth in their thinking skills and metacognitive processes.

Assessment For Learning

Assessment For Learning is the process of *"seeking and interpreting evidence for use by learners and their teachers to decide where the learners are in their learning, where they need to go and how best to get there"* (Broadfoot et al, 2002). It is a core part of everyday classroom practice by teachers, students and peers that *"seeks, reflects upon and responds to information from dialogue, demonstration and observation in ways that enhance ongoing learning"* (Klenowski, 2009).

True *Assessment For Learning* is the ongoing and embedded effort to understand our students' learning. It lives in our listening, observing, examining, analysing and reflecting on the process of learning. *Assessment For Learning*, however, only becomes formative when we use the data to inform our teaching and students' learning. It is driven by our curiosity about our students' learning and the desire to make sure our teaching is responsive to their needs as learners. If we want to know not just what our students know, but how they know it, then we must make their thinking visible (Ritchhart & Church, 2020).

The use of thinking routines in the classroom supports educators in gaining valuable insights into the critical and creative thinking skills of their students and their ability to apply those skills to support the understanding of key content and concepts. They are invaluable *Assessment For Learning* tools that help teachers better understand the individual learners in their classrooms, the types of learning and scaffolding required to further their learning and develop their thinking in a more effective way (Ritchhart & Church, 2020).

Combined with thinking routines, the use of Socratic questioning techniques to clarify and dig deeper into the critical and creative thought processes of students is an important part of understanding the thinking, perspectives and knowledge of the learners in our classrooms. It is also an effective way to encourage learners to inquire into their own thinking and explore more deeply what, how and why they think (Murdoch, 2015). Some examples of Socratic question stems that could be utilised in the classroom include:

	Example Socratic question stems
Clarify	<ul><li>What do you mean by…?</li><li>Can you elaborate further?</li><li>Can you give me an example?</li><li>Can you illustrate what you mean?</li><li>How does that connect with…?</li><li>Can you give me more details?</li></ul>
Probe assumptions	<ul><li>What makes you say that?</li><li>Can you elaborate on your thinking?</li><li>How could we find out if that is true?</li><li>How would we verify or test that?</li></ul>
Justify and seek evidence	<ul><li>Can you give me an example of…?</li><li>How do you know that…?</li><li>How could we check on that?</li><li>How might someone argue against…?</li><li>Can you support your thinking with evidence?</li><li>What would you need to change your thinking?</li></ul>
Elicit other perspectives and viewpoints	<ul><li>What's another way of looking at this?</li><li>If you were… what might you say/think/do?</li><li>How does this compare with…?</li><li>How does this fit with what you already know?</li><li>Do we need to look at this from another perspective or viewpoint?</li></ul>

Explore and reveal implications and consequences	<ul><li>So, if this is true, what would it mean for…?</li><li>What might that lead to?</li><li>What if this is not the case?</li><li>What would happen if…?</li><li>What lies beneath the surface of this?</li><li>What's at the core or centre of this?</li><li>What factors make this a difficult problem?</li></ul>
Think about the question itself	<ul><li>Why do you think this question is important?</li><li>Is there a better way of asking this?</li><li>If we asked the question this way, how would our thinking change?</li><li>What are some of the complexities of this question?</li></ul>

Table 1: Socratic questioning examples
(adapted from Paul & Elder, 2008; Murdoch, 2015)

Assessment As Learning

Assessment As Learning occurs when students are their own assessors. Students monitor their own learning, ask questions and use a range of strategies to decide what they know and can do, and how to use assessment information for new learning (NSW Education Standards Authority, n.d.). Skilled self-reflection and assessment can be as reliable as other forms of assessment; however, teachers must provide students with the necessary structures, scaffolds and environment in order to learn to become effective self-reflective learners. Demore highlights that self-reflection is *"the evaluation or judgement of one's performance and the identification of one's strengths and weaknesses with a view to improving one's learning outcomes"* (2017).

In the classroom, providing opportunities for students to learn and apply effective reflection on learning strategies is an essential component to the development of metacognition or 'thinking about thinking'. If we re-examine the ACARA Critical and Creative Thinking learning continuum from chapter 2, it is evident that 'reflecting on thinking and processes' is an important part of developing critical and creative thinkers in our classrooms, and highlights three key areas of development:

- Thinking about thinking (metacognition)
- Reflect on processes
- Transfer knowledge into new contexts

It is through this learning continuum that educators can develop an understanding of the types of *Assessment As Learning* practices they can typically expect their learners to be able to learn and demonstrate by the end of a given grade level, provided they have been exposed to explicit instruction and strategic scaffolding opportunities. Take, for example, the expectations for Kindergarten (sometimes referred to as Foundation or Prep in other states) and Year 10 students in the three areas:

- Thinking about thinking (metacognition)

    By the end of Kindergarten → *By the end of Year 10*
    Describe what they are thinking and give reasons why → Give reasons to support their thinking, and address opposing viewpoints and possible weaknesses in their own positions

- Reflect on processes

    By the end of Kindergarten → *By the end of Year 10*
    Identify the main elements of the steps in a thinking process → Balance rational and irrational components of a complex or ambiguous problem to evaluate evidence

- Transfer knowledge into new contexts

    By the end of Kindergarten → *By the end of Year 10*
    Connect information from one setting to another → Identify, plan and justify transference of knowledge to new contexts

Developing thinking requires that students are *"given time and opportunity to talk about thinking processes, to make their own thought processes more explicit, thus enabling them to clarify and reflect upon their strategies"* and become more self-regulated learners (McGuinness, 1999). The role of the critical friend is beneficial to learners and is supported through peer reflection or assessment practices. It is important for educators to remember that peer assessment requires explicit scaffolding for students as they learn to notice and name the learning and thinking of a peer and offer constructive feedback in relation to the success criteria for learning.

Assessment Of Learning

Assessment is vital to the teaching and learning process. In schools, the most visible forms of assessment are generally summative in nature and are used to measure what students have learnt at the end of a learning sequence, term or semester, in order to assess achievement against outcomes and standards (Organisation for Economic Co-operation and Development, 2008).

Assessment Of Learning is the assessment we do at the conclusion of a learning sequence and is a key indicator of impact, that is, the impact of teacher clarity, instruction and choice of experiences on the learning of all students and their demonstration of that learning in relation to outcomes and indicators of learning. It is often this form of assessment that educators use to provide evidence of achievement to the wider community and support the shaping of future learning goals and pathways for students (NSW Education Standards Authority, n.d.).

In addition to strong *Assessment Of Learning* practices, the use of the ACARA Critical and Creative Thinking learning continuum can support teachers in assessing the critical and creative thinking skills of their students against typical age markers. As students continue to grow and develop as learners and engage with increasingly complex subject matter, they develop better cognitive resources and are exposed to more experiences that encourage sophisticated thinking (Ellerton, 2017). Utilising the ACARA learning continuum to support understanding around students' development is considered to be a 'developmental' approach to assessment and as such, educators must ensure that it remains prescriptive rather than descriptive so as to keep focused on what we wish for students to achieve as a result of targeted improvement (Ellerton, 2017).

Thinking routines as tools *For* and *As* assessment

Thinking routines are powerful vehicles through which we can make visible the thinking of our students. They are a valuable tool for assessing the thinking skills and understanding of our students and as such support other formative and summative assessment practices that are woven into the teaching and learning cycle. Ritchhart and Church highlight in the book *The Power of Making Thinking Visible* that thinking routines should not be assigned a score or value as *"doing so will quickly send a message that you are looking for a specific answer rather than their thinking"* (2020).

Rather, it is through noticing, naming, observing, questioning and examining that teachers are able to make informed judgements about where students are at and where their learning needs to go moving forward. Take, for example, the thinking routines that were highlighted in part three (The thinking classroom in action). Here are some examples of how you might use these routines as part of ongoing assessment in the classroom, with deepening responses occurring over time.

Thinking routine	How can I use this routine as an assessment?
See Think Wonder (pages 82 and 109)	- Are students able to notice details that take them deeper into the stimulus rather than getting stuck on immediate surface features? - What kind of supports or evidence are students able to provide to support their interpretations? - Are they drawing on evidence to create coherent links? - Are students asking more adventurous and broad questions or are they limited to those requiring specific factual responses? **Type of assessment:** - *Assessment For Learning*
Main Side Hidden (page 87)	- Can learners identify the main character and the events that take place for this character? - Are learners able to recognise and identify supporting characters? - Are they able to identify the story that is occurring for one or more supporting characters? - Can they identify the hidden message or theme of the story? - Does the learner identify contextual clues to support their thinking? **Type of assessment:** - *Assessment For Learning* - Supports *Assessment Of Learning* experiences
Step Inside (page 91)	- Are students able to identify important details from the perspective of the focus character? - Can the learner make informed inferences and hypothesise what might be happening? - Are they aware of the complexities of what someone may feel or care about? - Are they able to draw on contextual clues to support this? - Are responses calling for inference based on evidence and reason? - Can the student build a plausible case for the positions they advocate? - Are they able to create a rich and full sense of a character using the ideas generated from the routine? **Type of assessment:** - *Assessment For Learning* - Supports *Assessment Of Learning* experiences

Peel the Fruit (page 95)	- Are students able to notice details that take them deeper into the stimulus rather than getting stuck on immediate surface features? - Are learners able to explain what it is really about in a deeper way or is their explanation only scratching the surface? - Can learners make connections beyond themselves and their own experiences? - Do learners identify different viewpoints and consider the topic, issue or text from the perspective of another? - Are learners able to recognise the central theme or message being conveyed? **Type of assessment:** - *Assessment For Learning* - Supports *Assessment Of Learning* experiences
Claim Support Question (page 102)	- Do learners recognise when suggestions have been made or explanations have been given that seem too broad-stroked to go unchallenged? - Are they looking for the generalisations and conjectures that get to the truth of an event? - What strategies are students adopting to assess the validity of claims? - When learners offer support for a given claim, is it anchored in solid evidence? - Do they recognise questions that need addressing in order to fully comprehend the complexity? **Type of assessment:** - *Assessment For Learning*
I used to think… Now I think… (page 106)	- Do students make mention of particular concepts or a new skill they have acquired? - Do students mention shifts in their thinking about key ideas either expected or unexpected? - Are students able to identify what they need to do next to further support their learning? **Type of assessment:** - *Assessment For Learning* - *Assessment As Learning*
Connect Extend Challenge (page 114)	- How are learners making sense of ongoing, collective ideas through connections and extensions they share? - Are they able to recognise particular themes or nuances that tie ideas together? - Are students seeing how ideas and concepts explored in the topic are connected to or have relevance to bigger ideas in other subjects or beyond school? **Type of assessment:** - *Assessment For Learning* - *Assessment As Learning*

Think Puzzle Explore (page 122)	• What key ideas and concepts do students already know? • Are they able to articulate clearly their current understanding? • What misconceptions are evident in students' current thinking? • What ideas are students interested in exploring further? • Are students able to express broad curiosities or are questions specific to short, factual responses? • Are students able to identify the connections between questions posed? • Can students categorise key questions to form a larger inquiry focus? • Are students able to combine and reword questions to develop questions with a broader curiosity? **Type of assessment:** • *Assessment For Learning*	
Chalk Talk (page 128)	• Are students able to make relevant contributions and connections? • Are the contributions related to the big ideas or are they peripheral connections? • Are students able to put forth their own ideas and original thinking, or do they hang back and echo the responses of others? • Do the questions posed go to the heart and substance of the topic or are they tangential? • Are they building understanding by incorporating ideas and wonderings stated by others, or do they find it difficult to integrate ideas of other students? **Type of assessment:** • *Assessment For Learning*	
Plus One (page 131)	• Are students able to recall key pieces of information from memory? • Do they include detailed ideas or basic facts? • Are they able to add new ideas, elaborate and add detail to the ideas of others or identify connections between ideas on the pages of their peers? • Are the additions basic and simplistic or do they elaborate/add/connect using detailed responses often supported by evidence? **Type of assessment:** • *Assessment For Learning*	

Layered Inference (page 136)	• Are students able to identify key evidence and facts? • Do they include detailed ideas or basic facts? • Are they able to use prior knowledge to make inferences about missing information? • Are students able to identify questions they can use to explore concepts further? **Type of assessment:** • *Assessment For Learning*	
Generate, Sort, Connect, Elaborate (page 11)	• Are students able to differentiate between key ideas and peripheral ones? • Have they identified the most important ideas? • What does the elaboration on ideas tell you about the students' depth of conceptual understanding? • What sort of connections are they making? • Are they making connections that are less obvious and provide insight into the deep structure of ideas? **Type of assessment:** • *Assessment For Learning*	
The Explanation Game (page 179)	• Do they state the obvious or are students probing beneath the surface, stretching for connections and possible relationships? • Do explanations seem broad, or are they rich in detail, descriptive and evocative? • Do explanations capture important characteristics, themes and elements? • Are students able to provide reasons to support their explanations? • Are the reasons provided supported by evidence? • Can students provide plausible alternatives and solutions? **Type of assessment:** • *Assessment As Learning*	
4-Square Criterion Reflection (page 145)	• Are students able to identify the key success criterion points? • Can students make accurate judgements about their learning progress? • Do they identify evidence of learning to support their judgements? • Are students able to identify clear and specific learning goals? • Can they clearly articulate and provide constructive feedback to peers about their learning and areas for growth? **Type of assessment:** • *Assessment As Learning*	

3, 2, 1 Reflection (page 149)	• Are students able to recall key pieces of information from memory? • Do they include detailed ideas or basic facts? • Can students articulate further questions that support the learning already undertaken? • Are these broad curiosities or basic facts-focused questions? • Are students able to identify a learning challenge? • Are they specific and detailed in identifying the challenge or is it basic and ambiguous? • Can students articulate how they did or intend to overcome the identified challenge? **Type of assessment:** • *Assessment As Learning*
Traffic Light Reflection (page 151)	• What are you noticing about how readily students identify places of potential puzzles? • What do you notice about the reasons students provide for making particular choices? • Are students able to make accurate judgements about their learning progress? **Type of assessment:** • *Assessment As Learning*
Give 3 (page 154)	• Are learners able to articulate their thinking to their partner about a particular piece of work? • Can they identify aspects of a piece of work that meet the success criteria? • Can they engage in meaningful discussions with a peer about elements that need further explanation and clarity? • Can they justify their feedback responses? • Can they identify ways a piece of work might be improved and link this back to the success criteria? • Are they able to support this judgement with evidence from a worked example? **Type of assessment:** • *Assessment As Learning*

Table 2: Using thinking routines as assessment tools (adapted from Ritchhart et al, 2011)

Chapter reflection questions

After reading chapter 10, take a moment to reflect on your learning and understanding.

1. What opportunities do you provide that allows you to see and hear the thinking and wondering of your students?
2. What role does the type of questions educators ask play in the level of wondering we see from learners?
3. What is our impact on what we are seeing and hearing from students? How does this inform your practice?
4. How might thinking routines support the assessment practices you use in your classroom?
5. How might Socratic questioning techniques help you to dig deeper into the thought processes of your students?
6. How might the ACARA Critical and Creative Thinking learning continuum support educators in understanding where our students are going in terms of providing targeted improvement?
7. Use the following routine to reflect on your thinking and understanding so far:
    a. I used to think...

    b. Now I think...

    c. So next I will...

CHAPTER 11

How do we assess students' depth of understanding?

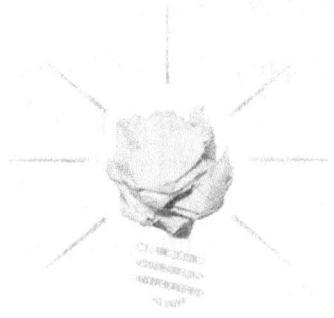

*"By asking students to make their thinking
visible through a thinking routine, I not only
can collect data about specific areas of learning
that I want to understand, but also am able
to reveal students' learning in ways that
I had not considered or anticipated"*

Katrin Robertson in The Power of Making Thinking Visible *(2020)*

The primary role of assessment is to establish where individuals are in their learning so that teaching can be differentiated, and further learning progress can be monitored over time. As educators, it is important that we understand and are able to recognise when students are working in the three different phases of learning – surface, deep and transfer – and support them to move through these phases, recognising that one is not more privileged than the other. In the classroom, this supports the decision-making process about *how* and *when* to engage students in certain tasks, questioning techniques and teaching strategies (Hattie, Fisher, Frey, Gojak, Moore & Mellman, 2016).

This chapter explores the notion of surface learning, deep understanding and transfer of understanding, and how teachers can recognise these phases and support students as they spiral through them, developing and consolidating their understanding and critical and creative thinking skills.

Chapter learning intentions

By the end of this chapter, educators will be able to:

- Identify the key components of the three phases of learning: surface, deep and transfer
- Explain ways to assess the depth of understanding and critical and creative thinking skills through the three phases of learning

Learning is a process and a consequence of thinking, not an event, and as such is comprised of three phases of learning: surface, deep and transfer. It would be convenient to argue that the three phases occur in a linear fashion and happen one after the other, but in reality, these three phases of learning spiral around one another across an ever-widening plane (Hattie, Fisher, Frey, Gojak, Moore & Mellman, 2016). Skilled teachers know that it is about getting the balance right between the three phases of learning, not a one-or-the-other-type mentality. Some things students only understand at the surface level, which is perfectly fine. You have to know something in order to be able to do something with it. With appropriate scaffolding and instruction on how to relate and extend ideas, surface learning becomes deep understanding.

Deep understanding is important if students are going to set their own expectations and monitor their own achievements. Learning also demands that learners be able to apply and transfer their knowledge, skills and strategies to new situations (Fisher, Frey & Hattie, 2016). In the classroom, it is about ensuring that students have the foundational knowledge and skills to be able to build a greater understanding before diving into those teaching and learning experiences. This is where the skilled art of differentiation is crucial. For example, a student is not going to be able to evaluate two pieces of literature if they do not yet have a foundational understanding of each text at a literal, structural and inferential level (Fisher, Frey & Hattie, 2016). Let's examine a brief overview of the three phases of learning.

Surface learning

Surface learning is the initiation to, and early understanding of, new ideas that begins with developing conceptual understanding before explicitly introducing further structure to concepts, such as labels and procedures, at the appropriate time. Research conducted by Hattie and colleagues highlights that the surface phase of learning comprises two parts: acquiring and consolidating (Hattie & Donoghue, 2016).

Acquiring surface learning
This component is focused on the initial learning of concepts and skills through an initial exploration or structured and explicit instruction. As Hattie et al highlight, when learning and content are new to students, it is expected that they will *"have a limited understanding. This does not mean that they are not working on complex problems; rather, the depth of thinking isn't there ye*t" (2016).

Consolidating surface learning
Taking surface learning beyond an introductory point of acquisition requires time and space to begin consolidating new learning. It is

through the process of consolidation that students begin to retrieve information efficiently so that they can make room for more complex problem-solving (Hattie, Fisher, Frey, Gojak, Moore & Mellman, 2016). Feedback plays a crucial role in helping students to consolidate their conceptual understanding and skills in order to be able to effectively support deeper learning.

It is through the development of surface learning that students have the opportunity to develop initial conceptual understandings, hone their thinking skills and begin to develop fluency with their skills in different curriculum areas. For example, surface learning strategies can be used to help students begin to develop their critical and creative thinking skills, such as their metacognitive processes. This phase of learning also provides educators with a great opportunity to address any misconceptions that students hold about a particular concept.

Deep understanding

Deep learning is focused on building a greater understanding of how ideas relate and connect to each other and extend to other understandings (Hattie, 2012). Often, this is accomplished through collaborative learning experiences with peers and opportunities to interact in richer ways with ideas and information. Referred to as the 'sweet spot', learning for deep understanding will often take up more instructional time, but can be accomplished only when students have the requisite knowledge to go deeper. This phase of learning is also comprised of two parts: acquiring and consolidating (Hattie & Donoghue, 2016).

Acquiring deep understanding
This component is about supporting students to plan, investigate and elaborate on their conceptual understandings, moving towards making generalisations. Through intentional and explicit instruction, skilled educators support and enable students to see how their conceptual understanding links to more efficient and flexible ways of thinking about a concept.

Consolidating deep understanding

This component focuses on the students' ability to utilise learning strategies that support them in consolidating deeper thinking as they become more strategic about their learning. It is through consolidation that we can determine the extent to which conceptual understandings have become part of the repertoire of skills and strategies a learner is able to employ in an 'automatised' way. At a deep level, students see connections, relationships and schema between ideas and learn to organise skills and concepts. Deep learning often involves interacting with peers and provides students with 'aha' moments as they discover these connections. It is the integration of ideas that signals the deep phase of learning (Frey, Hattie & Fisher, 2018).

Transfer of understanding

A transfer of understanding occurs when students are able to take their consolidated knowledge and skills and apply what they know to new scenarios and different contexts. It is also a time when students are able to think metacognitively, reflecting on their own learning and understanding. This is considered the ultimate goal of learning, and one that educators work hard to realise for all of their students. The notion of transfer of understanding into learning is both a goal and also a vehicle for propelling learning forward. This is where our learners begin to take the reins of their own learning, think metacognitively and apply what they know to a variety of real-world contexts (Hattie, Fisher, Frey, Gojak, Moore & Mellman, 2016). When students begin to apply knowledge in increasingly new and novel situations, the transfer level of learning is reached. To our thinking, transfer is the goal of learning. When students reach the point of transfer, they own the concept or skill and know how to use it (Frey, Hattie & Fisher, 2018).

Connecting it to classroom practice

As educators, it is our goal to find the balance with the three phases of learning in the classroom. This ongoing and continuous spiral means that we must be strategic, explicit, reflective and intentional with the choices of learning experiences we provide and the way in which we scaffold the thinking skills of our students through these learning experiences. As Hattie and colleagues highlight:

> "What *and* when *are equally important when it comes to instruction that has an impact on learning. Approaches that facilitate students' surface-level learning do not work equally well for deep learning, and vice versa. Matching the right approach with the appropriate phase of learning is the critical lesson to be learned."*
> (Hattie, Fisher, Frey, Gojak, Moore & Mellman, 2016)

When we utilise thinking routines and questioning techniques to promote the thinking of our students and the development of their conceptual understandings, it is essential that we choose the right 'thinking tool' for the job. Therefore, we must first identify the phase of learning the learners are at and the type of thinking we are trying to elicit from our students in order to have the greatest impact on student learning. This allows educators to recognise the types of responses they are trying to elicit from the beginning, and notice, name and make anecdotal observations about the responses and justifications being provided by the students. Combined with an understanding of the phases of thinking development (refer back to chapter 4, figure 11), educators are able to utilise thinking routines to strategically scaffold and support students as they transition in and out of the phases of learning. The thinking routines we have shared in this book thus far are valuable tools teachers can draw on to support the critical and creative thinking skills of their students.

Take, for instance, the thinking routine Layered Inference (page 136). This routine can be a valuable tool to support students as they learn about a concept, make connections and inferences, and use reflection and questioning to drive future learning. When students are working in the surface learning phase, responses to the stimulus piece that is linked to a broader conceptual understanding might be basic or show small pieces of connected prior knowledge. As an educator, this supports the development of future learning experiences that help to support and build understanding through a layered meaning approach. As students engage further in learning experiences explicitly structured to support their conceptual understanding, the use of the Layered Inference routine with the same or similar stimulus should reveal greater ideas, connections between ideas and consolidation of understanding about the concept. This also provides a rich opportunity for students to engage in *Assessment As Learning* practices to reflect on their growth as a learner in both conceptual understanding and metacognitive processes.

The Explanation Game

Let's take a look at another thinking routine called The Explanation Game, adapted from Ritchhart, Church and Morrison (2011). This thinking routine enables learners to look closely at key features and important details of a stimulus, generate explanations supported by evidence and provide reasons for their thinking. This thinking routine is separated into four components:

- **Name it:** Students notice, name and record all of the components they have observed about the stimulus.
- **Explain it:** Students generate multiple explanations about the features identified in the stimulus.
- **Give reasons:** Students generate reasons to support why their explanation is plausible. Probe deeper with the prompt *What have you seen that makes you say that?*
- **Generate alternatives:** Students develop alternative explanations than the initial ones with the goal of focusing on the relationship between the features and why they are that way.

Activity: The Explanation Game and the phases of learning

Choose one or more of the thinking routines that have been examined so far. Use The Explanation Game thinking routine prompts to explore how the chosen thinking routine(s) might support students as they spiral through the phases of learning: surface, deep and transfer.

	Surface learning	Deep understanding	Transfer of understanding
Focus thinking routine			
Name it Identify the features of the routine			
Explain it Explain how these features support the identified phase of learning			
Give reasons Provide reasons as to why you believe they support that phase of learning. What have you seen that makes you say that?			
Generate alternatives Identify the relationship between the features and how it supports the phase of learning. How else might we explain it?			

Table 3: Phases of learning in The Explanation Game thinking routine

Scan the QR code to find out more about the The Explanation Game thinking routine.

Chapter reflection questions

After reading chapter 11, take a moment to reflect on your learning and understanding.

1. What are the key features or components of each phase of learning?
   a. Surface learning
   b. Deep understanding
   c. Transfer of understanding
2. How do you currently support the three phases of learning in the classroom?
3. How do thinking routines help educators to support students through the three phases of learning?
4. After reflecting on your practice, use the start, repeat, delete practitioner reflection to set some professional goals.
   a. **Start:** What is one new thing you will start trialling or adding to your practice?
   b. **Repeat:** What is one thing that you have found impactful that you will continue with?
   c. **Delete:** What is one thing you are going to stop doing and remove from your practice?

CHAPTER 12

How do we utilise the SOLO Taxonomy to shift student thinking?

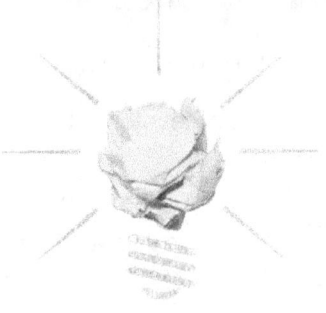

"Do we measure what is valuable, or simply value what is measurable?"

Corinna Wells

As students engage with learning experiences and broaden their conceptual understandings, the learning process becomes more complex. So, too, does the need for educators to differentiate instruction, feedback and learning experiences based on a strong understanding of where students are at currently and where they are headed in the learning journey. Utilising a framework to pinpoint how a student's thinking and conceptual understanding is progressing and the phase of learning a student is currently operating at has not only benefits for the teacher's pedagogical practice, but also for students' learning. SOLO, which stands for the *Structure of the Observed Learning Outcome*, is a means of classifying learning outcomes in terms of their complexity, enabling us to assess students' work in terms of its *quality* not of how many bits of this and of that they have got right (Biggs & Collis, 1981). This chapter explores the SOLO Taxonomy model and unpacks ways teachers can utilise it to measure thinking and depth of understanding in students' learning samples.

> **Chapter learning intentions**
>
> By the end of this chapter, educators will be able to:
>
> - Understand the range of levels in the SOLO Taxonomy model
> - Explain how the SOLO model can be used to support critical and creative thinking in the classroom

Unpacking the levels of the SOLO Taxonomy

The SOLO Taxonomy provides a simple, reliable and robust model for educators to identify and understand the three phases of learning – surface, deep and transfer – in student learning samples. It provides the criteria for assessing the cognitive complexity of students' understanding when mastering new learning; it was developed by Biggs and Collis in 1981. As the SOLO Taxonomy is not reliant on specific content, it is considered a generic measure that can be used by *"educators validly and reliably to identify ascending cognitive complexity in individual and collective student learning outcomes"*

(Hook, 2006). The SOLO Taxonomy model describes five levels of student understanding when encountering new learning:

- Prestructural
- Unistructural
- Multistructural
- Relational
- Extended abstract

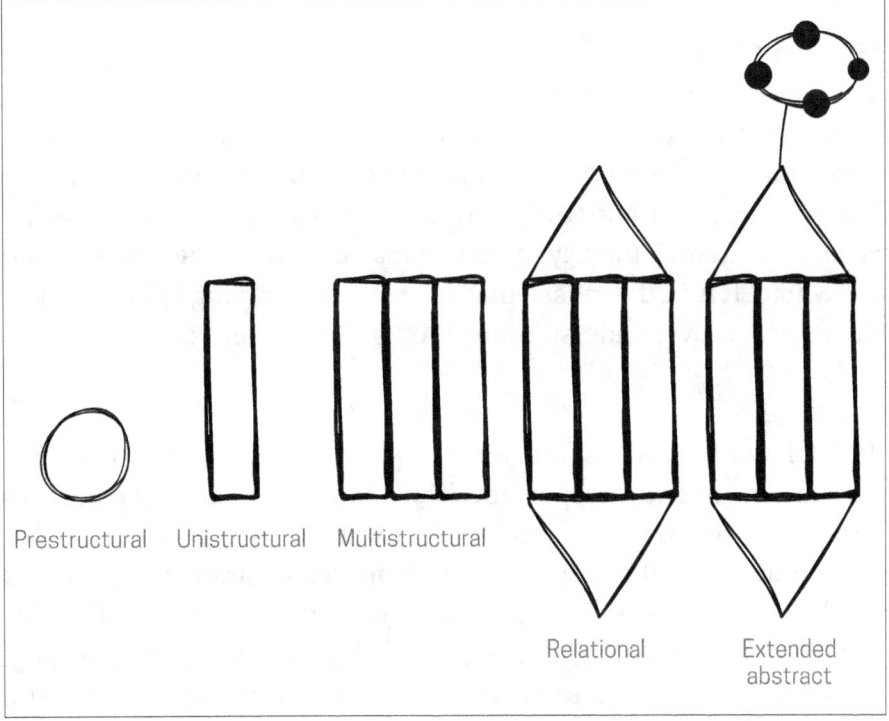

Figure 54: SOLO Taxonomy model (Hook, 2011)

The five levels are described as:

Prestructural
The prestructural level is the first and most basic level of response, which indicates that a student has not yet grasped the learning intention. The student working at this phase inappropriately attacks the task and their learning artifact highlights that they have limited understanding or require substantial help to begin the task (Wells, 2015; Hook, 2011).

Unistructural

The unistructural level is the ability to list or name one obvious factor with only a surface level of understanding. The student working at this phase picks up on one aspect of the task with disconnected or basic understanding. It is in this phase that students begin to acquire surface level understanding by bringing in one idea that they are able to work with, in order to build foundational understanding (Wells, 2015; Hook, 2011).

Multistructural

The multistructural level is where one or more factors are listed or named but without an understanding of interrelations and a developing level of understanding. The student working in this phase is able to recognise and work with several aspects of the task, but is not yet able to identify the key relationships between the key aspects and the whole. It is in this phase that students are working to consolidate their surface level understanding (Wells, 2015; Hook, 2011).

Relational

The relational level is the ability to integrate factors to form a conclusion and a deeper level of understanding. The student working at this phase identifies clear links between aspects and is able to integrate them. They are able to demonstrate a deeper and more coherent understanding of the concept as a whole. It is in this phase that students begin to acquire and consolidate a deep level of understanding through their ability to make connections (Wells, 2015; Hook, 2011).

Extended abstract

The extended abstract level is where understanding has progressed to a point where a person is able to conceptualise, hypothesise, critique, predict or reflect on information or factors that were not explicitly outlined. Students working at this phase demonstrate the ability to capture the new understanding at the relational level and rethink it at another conceptual level, examining it in new ways and extending ideas. It is in this phase that students are able to transfer their understanding to new contexts and develop a strong conceptual understanding (Wells, 2015; Hook, 2011).

Using the SOLO Taxonomy to assess thinking

The SOLO Taxonomy model is a useful tool for both teachers and students to identify where they 'are currently at' with their thinking and where the instructional strategies are trying to move their thinking to. Hattie explains that "*the model highlights the importance of knowing something (phase 2 and 3) before thinking about it. SOLO values the deep, but notes that students need time to master the foundations*" (Hattie, 2012). Assessment information provided by SOLO has implications for instruction. It offers the potential glue that can help teachers achieve the synchronisation of the three arms of the curriculum:

- Assessment
- Pedagogy
- Syllabus content

For educators, using a rubric or scale to support the analysis of student learning artifacts is a great way to pinpoint where a learner is working at across any curriculum area and the type and depth of critical and creative thinking skills being applied to a particular task at that point in time. If you are using a template, such as a thinking routine template, you might include the rubric on the template you are working with. Alternatively, if students are working in their subject area books, they might glue in the rubric underneath their work to support the analysis.

The following template is just one snapshot of how you might identify the phase of learning a student is working at and where they need to go next in their learning. The important thing to remember is that it needs to:

a. Give you the information you are looking for in terms of depth of understanding and the critical and creative thinking skills students are applying to the content
b. Be easy for you and your students to pick up and use
c. Be used consistently by the teacher as well as a reflection tool for the students
d. Be easy to interpret
e. Be clear and concise – not onerous to complete for each student

Learning intention:				
Level of critical and creative thinking				
Prestructural	Unistructural	Multistructural	Relational	Extended abstract

No idea	One idea	Multiple ideas but no connections	Multiple ideas with links and connections	Relational and able to think in new ways
Learning artifact observation:				

Figure 55: SOLO Taxonomy rubric example (adapted from Hook, 2011)

Take, for instance, the Layered Inference thinking routine student learning artifact. This learning artifact shows the depth of a Year 6 student's thinking during a history lesson where students were asked to examine a historical image depicting the Australian goldfields and explore the information that can be gathered about life on the goldfields at that point in history.

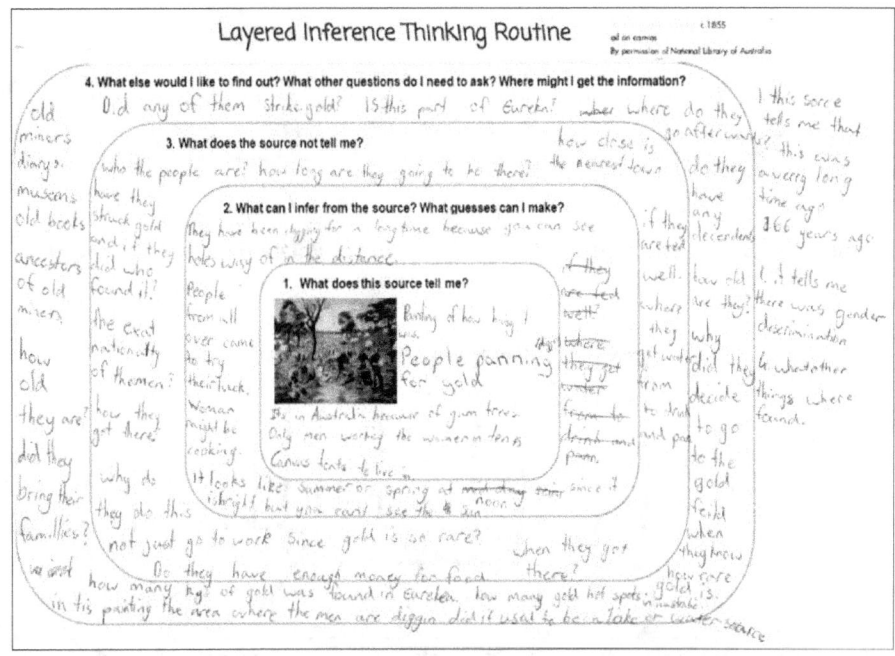

Figure 56: Layered Inference thinking routine student example

If we were to utilise the SOLO Taxonomy rubric to analyse the quality of information represented on this learning artifact, rather than simply observing the 'quantity' of ideas listed, it might be represented in the following way.

Learning intention:

To describe life on the Australian goldfields and explain why this period of time is significant in Australia's history.

Level of critical and creative thinking				
Prestructural	**Unistructural**	**Multistructural**	**Relational**	**Extended abstract**
 ○	 ▯	 ▯▯▯	 ◇▯	 ⬭◇▯
No idea	One idea	Multiple ideas but no connections	Multiple ideas with links and connections	Relational and able to think in new ways

Learning artifact observation:

This learning artifact highlights a student working at the relational level. They have consolidated their understanding of the factors that contributed to life on the goldfields, such as leaving families behind and living in tent cities, along with information that is not evident through viewing this artwork. The student is able to make connections to the significant event of the Eureka Stockade and the role of women in society at the time. The student mentions gender discrimination as being evident but no further elaborations are provided to support this thinking.

Figure 57: SOLO Taxonomy rubric worked example (adapted from Hook, 2011)

Learning intention

The learning in the rubric helps to keep focus on the intent of learning in order to keep the focus of analysing the learning artifact on the intention and purpose. To scale things up, you could also include the success criteria with the learning intention so that you can deepen the analysis against the measures of success.

Levels of critical and creative thinking

This component of the rubric acts as a reminder of the phases of the SOLO Taxonomy framework and keep them front and centre through the analysis of learning. Pamela Hooks' interpretation of the framework's images ensures that the key components of each phase are signalled visually (2011). The phase of learning a student is at could be highlighted or circled to show what this example highlights.

Learning artifact observation

This component of the rubric is where the Learning Intention of the task and SOLO Taxonomy phases really intersect. It is in this section that the teacher really drills down and highlights what the learning artifact demonstrates and potentially what is needed to take learning to that next level. It is here that the teacher is able to gauge the depth of understanding of a student in relation to the task and how they are connecting this to syllabus content and their own prior knowledge.

Through teacher modelling and explicit use of the SOLO Taxonomy rubric to analyse student learning artifacts and provide feedback about where a student is working at and where they are going next, this rubric forms a great way to support students to become self-reflective of their own learning. Students could use the same rubric the teacher uses, or for younger grades they may use a more simplified version with images only to support the *Assessment As Learning* process.

Using the SOLO Taxonomy framework to move learning forward

One of the great benefits to utilising the SOLO Taxonomy framework in the classroom alongside the SOLO Taxonomy rubric is the ability to pinpoint the students' depth of understanding and the where to next in the learning journey. Take, for instance, if a student is working at the following SOLO phases, as a teacher we might look for and ask the following questions:

The phase the student currently demonstrates	What the teacher might look for	Questions the teacher might ask to shift learning
Prestructural	<ul><li>Does the student know any relevant information?</li><li>What experiences might the student have that relate to this concept?</li></ul>	<ul><li>Can you tell me one thing that you can see, hear, identify, name?</li><li>Can you tell me about this?</li></ul>
Unistructural	<ul><li>Does the student's learning artifact show one relevant descriptive piece of information?</li></ul>	<ul><li>Can you tell me something else you can see, hear, identify or name?</li><li>Can you identify or name one additional feature?</li><li>How would you describe it?</li></ul>
Multistructural	<ul><li>Does the student's learning artifact show several descriptive pieces of information?</li><li>Is the student response mainly descriptive?</li></ul>	<ul><li>How might these ideas link to each other?</li><li>What makes you say that?</li><li>What key words are important here?</li></ul>

Relational	- Does the student's learning artifact use key syllabus terminology for this stage of learning? - Are causal relationships evident? - Does the student response show clear cause and effect with relevant language?	- You have identified strong links using key terminology to explain your thinking. How could you apply this thinking to a similar context?
Extended abstract	- Does the student learning artifact show relational understanding and show links to other relevant contexts? - How well does the student work sample relate to other ideas, both familiar and unfamiliar, to the student?	- You have clearly linked ideas and shown how they can be connected across contexts. How might you explain these connections to a different audience?

Table 4: SOLO Taxonomy and moving learning forward (adapted from Hook, 2011)

Chapter reflection questions

After reading chapter 12, take a moment to reflect on your learning and understanding.

1. How does the SOLO Taxonomy framework support teachers to understand the depth of student understanding?
2. How might the SOLO Taxonomy framework and the use of a rubric help the teacher to assess student work samples in relation to student levels of achievement?
3. How might you adapt the SOLO Taxonomy rubric for your classroom or school context?
4. Why do you think it is important that teachers understand the level of understanding that a task demands of students?

PART FIVE

LEADING TEAMS IN CRITICAL AND CREATIVE THINKING

CHAPTER 13

How do I support my team to embed critical and creative thinking in their practice?

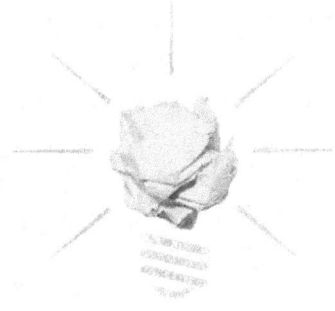

"Creating the conditions in schools and learning settings where curiosity is encouraged, developed and sustained is essential to opening up thinking, changing practice and creating dramatically more innovative approaches to learning and teaching"

Timperley, Kaser and Halbert (2014)

As a leader, it can seem overwhelming to support a team in embedding critical and creative thinking in their learning spaces – but the rewards are plentiful. Supporting teams of teachers in embedding critical and creative thinking into their classrooms requires an action inquiry mindset. It requires teams to be curious about the learning of their students and the shared goal of moving learning forward for all students based on data and consistent teacher judgement.

This chapter explores ways in which educators that lead a team of teachers can utilise the principals and practices that underpin critical and creative thinking to support and build the capacity of their team to effectively implement and build these skills in their students, through utilising key strategies, action inquiry models and data-informed conversations.

Chapter learning intentions

By the end of this chapter, educators will be able to:

- Understand the need to develop an action inquiry/ research process with their team
- Explain the role of collaboration in collectively building a culture of critical and creative thinking
- Identify how thinking routines can be used to examine and analyse data and student learning samples

Effectively leading a team is challenging work and requires a good understanding of the people you are working with, their strengths and areas for growth. A team is 'a number of persons associated together in work or activity', however, putting people in the same room or on the same grade together does not make them an effective team nor a collaborative one. Leaders must draw on strategies, protocols and frameworks in order to build the collaborative expertise, capacity and collective efficacy of their team and keep at the core a focus on improving student outcomes. Leading colleagues to embed critical and creative thinking into classrooms requires leaders to:

- Build a shared and common language
- Develop shared norms and expectations
- Build a common and collective focus and vision
- Explicitly use and model thinking routines
- Engage in data-informed conversations
- Support the connection of theory into practice
- Deliver professional development that is individualised to the needs of the teachers working within the team
- Ensure critical reflection flows through the phases of an action inquiry cycle
- Draw upon an action inquiry framework to develop a consistent cycle of inquiry into teaching and learning practices

Embedding a framework

Utilising a framework to support teaching teams to engage in action inquiry and bridge the gap between theory and practice is essential to building the capacity of staff and improving student learning outcomes. There are lots of different models that leaders can draw upon, such as Spiral of Inquiry, Teaching Sprints, Collaborative Data Inquiry and Action Research (Timperley, Kaser & Halbert, 2014; Breakspear & Jones, 2020; Boudett, City & Murnane, 2013; Mertler, 2016)

An action inquiry cycle is one framework that I draw upon when leading teachers to build critical and creative thinking capabilities in and with their students. It is through this cycle that I work collaboratively with my team to embed evidence-based and data-informed practices in classrooms.

Figure 58: Action inquiry cycles

The action inquiry cycle framework is comprised of four key components:

1. Action planning
2. Implementation
3. Professional learning
4. Review and impact

This framework is cyclical in nature, whereby progress towards growth in student critical and creative thinking and learning is made in small chunks. It is a process that is informed by evidence, whether that be through a data set or student learning samples or artifacts. What is crucial is that this process remains focused on student learning and identifying student areas for growth and development. The norms and habits of mind you co-develop and agree to when you organise for collaborative work will help you stay focused on taking action to change your practice (Boudett, City & Murnane, 2013).

Action planning

The action planning phase of the inquiry cycle is about collaboratively analysing data or student learning artifacts in order to identify a learner-centred problem that can be addressed through utilising instructional practices. As a leader, it is in this phase of the framework that we work with teachers to examine a learning artifact to make consistent judgements about the critical and creative thinking capabilities of the students, the type of thinking a task is requiring of students and where we want student thinking to go moving forward. It is in this phase that leaders can draw upon thinking routines to help guide conversations around data, such as:

See Think Wonder

This routine helps leaders to focus the exploration of data or learning artifacts on what can be observed and limit the amount of inference teachers make about why particular data/artifacts are the way they are. As we have explored across a number of chapters already, the See Think Wonder thinking routine is comprised of three components and it is these same three prompts that guide the discussion with teachers. It is important to provide teaching teams time to independently examine the data set or learning artifact first before engaging in discussions about it.

- *What do you see, observe or notice?*
  It is through this question that leaders ask teachers to think about all the observable elements to the data or learning artifact, focusing the conversation purely on the facts and eliminating the 'why' behind the data. This is important as we want to reduce climbing the 'ladder of inference' and attaching blame or excuses to the data (Boudett, City & Murnane, 2013).

- *What do you think...*
  - *...are the observable strengths?*
    This question focuses the discussion on the areas of celebration in the data set or learning artifact. Too often, as teachers and leaders, we jump to what is concerning us and forget to celebrate the achievement of students and the instructional

strategies that were used to support this achievement. Being able to identify the observable strengths also allows for deeper reflection around what worked and who benefitted from this instruction (Fisher, Frey, Almarode, Flories & Nagel, 2019).

- *...are the areas for growth?*
  This question focuses the discussion on areas that teachers can have the greatest instructional impact and see the greatest growth through a consolidation of skills, knowledge and understanding. It is through this prompt that teachers can begin to identify areas for future explicit instruction or continued exposure and practice.

- *...are the areas of concern?*
  This question focuses the discussion on the 'big red flags' that arise in the data set or learning artifact. It is through this prompt that leaders can begin to unpack the 'why' behind the areas of concern. Perhaps there was an inconsistent approach to explicit instruction, perhaps the concept was only taught incidentally or there is a lack of teacher confidence or certainty in developing these skills in students. This discussion allows the leader to focus their support and offer professional development opportunities to build the capacity of the team to confidently and explicitly address the needs of students.

- *What do you wonder?*
  It is through this question that leaders ask teachers to consider any wonderings they may currently have about the data. Perhaps there is an anomaly present in the data set or learning artifact that in the classroom doesn't present as an issue but is being observed currently in the data. This is the perfect opportunity in the discussion to consider if additional data is required to create a deeper understanding about what is truly occurring for learners and their thinking or if our 'hunches' can be triangulated across multiple sources.

It is from this data-focused discussion that, as a leader, I am able to shift attention to the identification of a problem of practice that is focused on the students and helping them to achieve growth in their thinking and learning capabilities. In a Collaborative Data Inquiry approach this is termed a learner-centred problem, which is fitting as we want the focus of these collaborative discussions with our teams to be focused on our learners and where they are at (Boudett, City & Murnane, 2013). What we look for and discuss is areas of growth or concern in the learning artifacts/data that is considered a consistent problem across the majority of learners. This helps to keep the focus on the learners rather than on what teachers are or are not doing.

Once this problem of practice has been identified, leaders engage their team in a discussion about the instructional practices, structures and scaffolds that could be employed to address the learner-centred problem. For example, a problem of practice might be that *students are having difficulties building explanations about [x]* with a focus on explicit teaching of explanation skills and utilising thinking routines such as the Generate, Sort, Connect, Elaborate concept map to support the development, consolidation, application and transference of the core thinking skill.

Collaboratively planning instructional strategies, tasks and resources with the team helps to ensure consistent language and pedagogical approaches are used by all members of the team. This helps to build not only individual efficacy, but the collective efficacy of the team as it strives to improve outcomes for all students, not just those within their immediate classroom. Identification of who is responsible for what in the action plan, when and where it will occur and how we will measure impact through different forms of assessment along the way are also crucial components to the planning process.

Implementation

The implementation phase of the action inquiry cycle is where the team sets about putting the plan developed in phase one into action. This phase may vary in length, but typically might last anywhere between three to five weeks. The length of time the team works to change pedagogical practice and shift learning outcomes is important. It signals to the team that this is an ongoing commitment that will take time to implement and see the impact of.

In supporting teachers to embed critical and creative thinking capabilities in the classroom with their students, this is the phase in which the leader gets their hands dirty, so to speak. It is where the leader spends time with each member of their team, explicitly modelling, scaffolding and embedding the use of thinking routines so that teachers feel comfortable in being able to implement the key critical and creative thinking strategies and scaffolds required to move thinking and learning forward. It also supports the development of consistent understanding and practice embedded across the team. Although professional learning is included as a stand-alone phase, the reality is that during implementation the leader and teachers engage in ongoing professional learning to build their capacity and strengthen the teaching and learning cycle.

Engaging in key assessment or review checkpoints along the way helps teaching teams to remain focused on the goal of the action inquiry and determine the impact that the instructional strategies are having on the thinking and learning of students. This could take the form of:

- A pre-assessment at the beginning of the cycle
- *Assessment For Learning* and *Assessment As Learning* along the way
- Identification of the SOLO Taxonomy levels in learning samples
- *Assessment Of Learning* after a set period of time has elapsed after the action inquiry cycle
- Post-assessment to make comparative judgements about impact

Professional learning

The professional learning phase of the action inquiry cycle occurs throughout each of the other three phases, as it is about recognising, as a leader, opportunities to build the capacity of individual teachers within the teaching team to deliver evidence-based, data-informed instructional strategies in the classroom. It is important that leaders respect and recognise the strengths of each of their teaching team so as to draw on the expertise of other teachers to support the collective goal of the group. This empowers teachers to support others, support students beyond their classroom and widen their sphere of influence, which contributes to the collective efficacy of the team as it works to achieve growth in student thinking and learning. As such, there are a variety of ways that teachers can engage in professional development with the support of their leader during an action inquiry cycle, including:

- Instructional coaching
- Peer mentoring
- Co-teaching
- Classroom observations
- Professional learning courses
- Book study
- Educational readings
- Webinars
- Podcasts

While this list is not exhaustive, it provides leaders with a snapshot into ways that different forms of professional learning can be utilised to build the capacity of teachers depending on their identified learning needs.

Review and impact

The review and impact phase of the action inquiry cycle occurs at the culmination of a five-week process and is a time to critically reflect on the cycle that has occurred and collaboratively review the learner-centred problem, the goals, instructional strategies and measures of impact to determine the effectiveness of the cycle. During this phase of the cycle, the guiding question of *Who benefitted and who did not?* which underpins a professional learning community approach, is extremely useful in unpacking the evidence of impact and the call to action moving beyond this cycle (Fisher, Frey, Almarode, Flories & Nagel, 2019).

Answering these questions can be undertaken through examination of data sets, observational notes and student learning artifacts to ascertain the impact of instruction on critical and creative thinking skills. It is in this phase that leaders can draw upon thinking routines to help guide conversations around thinking and learning growth and impact, such as:

Claim Support Question

This routine is a useful tool for leaders to guide the discussion around impact in order to distinguish between who benefitted from instructional practices and who did not benefit, and why not. As we explored in chapter 7, which focused on thinking routines in numeracy, this routine has three key components, and it is these same three prompts that guide the discussion with teachers.

- *Make a claim*
  It is here that leaders might make a statement or claim about the data sets or learning artifacts at the conclusion of the action inquiry cycle. These statements generally identify observable patterns, highlight generalisations or identify assertions that will assist the team in identifying who benefitted and who did not. The claim should be directly related to the learner-centred problem identified in the planning phase of the action inquiry plan.

- *Identify supports for the claim*
  This component is about identifying and highlighting the evidence to support the claim or statement as well as raising the evidence that contradicts the claim to address multiple perspectives. This is where the focused discussion on who benefitted and who did not is undertaken, supported by the evidence.

- *Raise questions related to the claim*
  It is through this prompt that, as a leader, you delve into the 'why' behind the level of impact the instructional strategies, chosen learning experiences, support and professional learning have had on student growth and attainment of learning outcomes.

As a leader, this feeds nicely into the where to next part of the discussion where the teaching team begins a new action inquiry cycle through the discussion of possibilities, but also commits to action beyond the current cycle and a possible change or embedding of practice.

Action inquiry cycles operate in a cyclical fashion and are based on critical reflections undertaken by the teaching team along the journey, including a review and assessment of impact. They are a hugely beneficial way to build the team's capacity to identify, explicitly teach, model and scaffold the critical and creative thinking skills of both students and teaching teams. One of the practices that I find extremely useful to monitor, track and provide accountable to all team members is the use of a planning template. This template has been adapted from Collaborative Data Inquiry to suit the educational context within which I work (Boudett, City & Murnane, 2013). Through drawing upon a clear framework and through offering structure to collegial conversations, the action inquiry cycle allows groups to delve deeply into important issues, making the most of the valuable time we have as educators and ensuring that everyone's voice is heard and valued.

Action Inquiry Cycle			
Term	1 2 3 4		
Teaching term			
Our shared vision			
School improvement area			
Planning phase:			
Data set or learning artifact examined			
Areas of strength	**Areas for growth**		**Areas of concern**
Learner-centred problem			

Why is this an area needing to be addressed?
Instructional strategies

Implementation phase:

When	Task	Who	Where
When will it occur?	What tasks and activities are required to meet the desired outcome?	Who will undertake each task?	Where will it occur or be stored?

Plan to assess progress:

Time frame	Data Source	When	Goal
Short term			
Medium term			
Long term			

Review and impact:	
Who benefitted?	**Who did not benefit?**
Implications	
Call to action	

Table 5: Action inquiry cycle planning, implementation and review template

Chapter reflection questions

After reading chapter 13, take a moment to reflect on your learning and understanding.

1. What components of an action inquiry cycle do you and your team already have in place?
2. What components are you and your team going to work on implementing?
3. How might utilising an action inquiry plan assist you to lead the team in embedding critical and creative thinking?
4. How does modelling thinking routines help teachers to understand how to apply them in their own classrooms?

Conclusion

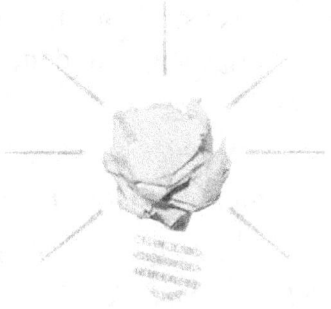

"Critical and creative thinking are the pillars on which we develop, consolidate and apply a conceptual understanding across the curriculum, and as such are critical skills all students must acquire"

Alice Vigors

Developing the critical and creative thinking skills of students in our classrooms is a necessary culture that all teachers should foster. Not only does it underpin the syllabus outcomes and content indicators across a range of state and national curriculums in Australia, but the skill of thinking critically and creatively, and being able to articulate that thinking to others is a hugely valuable skill to employers across a broad range of industries and professions. Building these skills and capabilities in our students need not be an onerous endeavour. In fact, many of the core practices highlighted throughout this book are possibly instructional and pedagogical practices that you already embed into the daily fabric of your classroom teaching.

Supporting students to be critical and creative thinkers requires us as educators to be willing to build our capacity, to make small consistent shifts towards embedding practices and fostering a 'thinking' environment that welcomes questions, that celebrates multiple perspectives and is comfortable working in a space that requires depth of understanding. As you critically reflect on where you are now and the type of thinking classroom you would like to create for your learners, it is important to take stock of what you've learnt, how this connects to what you already know and identify your where to from here. So, I ask you this:

What does fostering thinking look like in your classroom learning environment?

What small shift will you make towards building the critical and creative thinking capabilities of your students?

To assist you in being a self-reflective learner, I will guide you through one final reflective routine called Reflect, Start, Repeat, Delete that is perfect for examining your practice, breaking down what you will keep, what you will cease and what you will introduce (Teacher Takeaway Podcast, 2022). It is a reflective routine that is broken down into four components:

- Reflect
- Start
- Repeat
- Delete

Reflect

To begin, it is important to identify the connections we made and the growth in our own learning through generating a list using the guiding prompts:

- *What connections did you make to your own practice?*
- *What challenged your thinking?*
- *How was your understanding extended as a result of engaging with the book?*
- *What do you still wonder?*

Record your responses to these questions below.

Start

Think about something new you will begin doing or adding to your practice to support the critical and creative thinking capabilities of your students. Use the questioning prompts to guide your reflection:

- *What new practices, approaches or resources will you add to your classroom or to your leadership?*
- *What steps are required for implementation?*
- *How will you know it has been successful or impactful?*

Record your responses to these questions below.

Repeat

Think about the key pedagogical practices, structures and scaffolds that support the development of critical and creative thinking that have worked well for you that you want to continue to do moving forward. Use the questioning prompts to guide your reflection:

- *What practice, approach or resource is working well for you that you will continue to use in your classroom or leadership practice to foster critical and creative thinking skills?*
- *What do you think makes this work well?*
- *What impact is it having on your students and/or staff?*

Record your responses to these questions below.

Delete

Think about a pedagogical practice or structure that is not supporting the development of critical and creative thinking skills in the classroom. Use the questioning prompts to guide your reflection:

- *Why does this practice or structure inhibit the development of critical and creative thinking?*
- *Why do you think this might be?*
- *What do you hope to notice from removing this from your classroom or leadership practice?*

Record your responses to these questions below.

As much as fostering a culture of thinking and building the capabilities of our students to think critically and creatively is the universal goal of schooling, it is not as commonplace a practice that is embedded in the fabric of classrooms and discussed widely through action inquiry cycles as one might think or hope it to be. It is my hope that the classrooms of tomorrow begin to make small shifts towards developing a thinking classroom where students are aware of and can articulate different kinds of ways of thinking that is visible, valued and actively promoted.

It is my hope that teachers and leaders see the value in developing and consolidating surface-level understanding before delving deeper into more complex ways of thinking and knowing. My hope is an ambitious one, but it is certainly achievable, because students are curious beings, eager to learn about and understand the world around them, and what better profession to be in to help make that a reality for all students than that of education.

List of figures

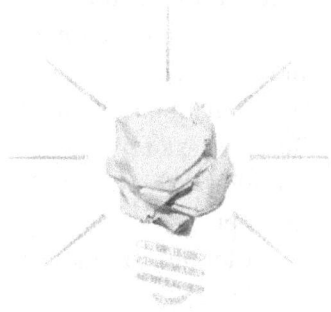

Figure 1:	GCSE concept map brainstorm example	13
Figure 2:	ACARA Critical and Creative Thinking learning elements	25
Figure 3:	Element: Inquiring: identifying, exploring and organising information and ideas	26
Figure 4:	Element: Generating ideas, possibilities and actions	28
Figure 5:	Element: Analysing, synthesising and evaluating reasoning and procedures	29
Figure 6:	Element: Reflecting on thinking and processes	30
Figure 7:	ACARA Critical and Creative Thinking learning continuum	32
Figure 8:	Principles of explicit instruction	38
Figure 9:	The gradual release of responsibility framework	43

Figure 10: Types of thinking routines (Ritchhart et al 2011)	53
Figure 11: Phases of thinking development	56
Figure 12: Bloom's Taxonomy of Critical Thinking Skills continuum (Hopkins & Craig, 2015)	63
Figure 13: Australian Professional Standards for Teachers (NSW Education Standards Authority, 2018)	67
Figure 14: Zoom In programme snapshot	70
Figure 15: Zoom In part I	72
Figure 16: Zoom In part II	73
Figure 17: Zoom In part III	74
Figure 18: Zoom In meets Main Side Hidden	75
Figure 19: Tug of War thinking routine (Ritchhart et al, 2011)	79
Figure 20: See Think Wonder thinking routine (adapted from Ritchhart et al, 2011)	83
Figure 21: Example of the See Think Wonder thinking routine in action	84
Figure 22: Main Side Hidden thinking routine (Ritchhart et al, 2011)	88
Figure 23: Main Side Hidden examples	90
Figure 24: Step Inside thinking routine (adapted from Ritchhart et al, 2011)	92
Figure 25: Step Inside thinking routine example	93
Figure 26: Peel the Fruit thinking routine (adapted from Ritchhart, 2020)	96
Figure 27: Peel the Fruit whole-class documentation example	97
Figure 28: Claim Support Question (adapted from Ritchhart et al, 2011)	103
Figure 29: Claim Support Question example	104
Figure 30: Claim Support Question whole-class documentation example	105
Figure 31: I used to think... Now I think... thinking routine (adapted from Ritchhart et al, 2011)	107
Figure 32: See Think Wonder thinking routine (adapted from Ritchhart et al, 2011)	109
Figure 33: See Think Wonder Mathematics prompt example	110
Figure 34: See Think Wonder Mathematics prompt example	112
Figure 35: Connect Extend Challenge thinking routine (adapted from Ritchhart et al, 2011)	115
Figure 36: Connect Extend Challenge example	118
Figure 37: Types of provocations	123
Figure 38: Think Puzzle Explore thinking routine (Ritchhart et al, 2011)	124
Figure 39: Think Puzzle Explore whole-class documentation example	125

Figure 40:	Programming and evaluation Think Puzzle Explore example	127
Figure 41:	Chalk Talk thinking routine (Ritchhart et al, 2011)	128
Figure 42:	Chalk Talk whole-class behaviour expectations example	130
Figure 43:	Plus One thinking routine (Ritchhart et al, 2020)	132
Figure 44:	Plus One thinking routine example	134
Figure 45:	Layered Inference thinking routine (Roberts, 2013)	137
Figure 46:	Layered Inference thinking routine example	138
Figure 47:	Phases of reflective thinking development (Vigors, 2019)	143
Figure 48:	4-Square Criterion Reflection thinking routine (adapted from Carroll, 2018)	146
Figure 49:	4-Square Criterion Reflection modelled example	147
Figure 50:	4-Square Criterion Reflection student example	148
Figure 51:	3, 2, 1 Reflection thinking routine (adapted from Ritchhart et al, 2011)	150
Figure 52:	Traffic Light Reflection thinking routine (adapted from Ritchhart et al, 2011)	152
Figure 53:	Give 3 feedback thinking routine (Vigors, 2019)	155
Figure 54:	SOLO Taxonomy model (Hook, 2011)	185
Figure 55:	SOLO Taxonomy rubric example (adapted from Hook, 2011)	188
Figure 56:	Layered Inference thinking routine student example	189
Figure 57:	SOLO Taxonomy rubric worked example (adapted from Hook, 2011)	190
Figure 58:	Action inquiry cycles	198

List of tables

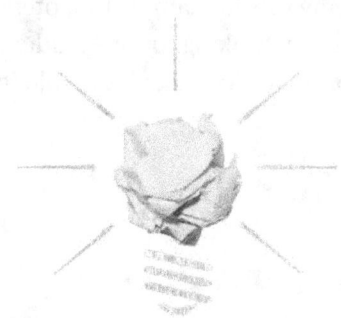

Table 1: Socratic questioning examples (adapted from Paul & Elder, 2008; Murdoch, 2015)   162

Table 2: Using thinking routines as assessment tools (adapted from Ritchhart et al, 2011)   167

Table 3: Phases of learning in The Explanation Game thinking routine   180

Table 4: SOLO Taxonomy and moving learning forward (adapted from Hook, 2011)   193

Table 5: Action inquiry cycle planning, implementation and review template   205

References

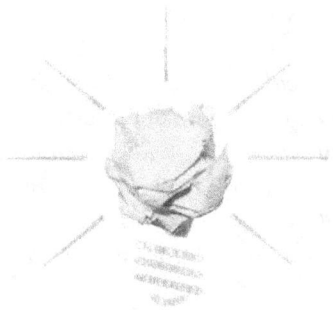

Alghafri, ASR, & Ismail, HNB (2014). 'The Effects of Integrating Creative and Critical Thinking on Schools Students' Thinking.' *International Journal of Social Science and Humanity*, Vol 4 (6), 518–525

Archer, AL, & Hughes, CA (2011). *Explicit instruction: Effective and Efficient Teaching*. Guilford Press

Australia Curriculum, Assessment and Reporting Authority (n.d.). 'Critical and Creative Thinking (Version 8.4).' Retrieved from www.australiancurriculum.edu.au/f-10-curriculum/general-capabilities/critical-and-creative-thinking/

Australian Institute for Teaching and School Leadership (2017). 'Learning Intentions and Success Criteria.' Retrieved from: www.aitsl.edu.au/docs/default-source/feedback/aitsl-learning-intentions-and-success-criteria-strategy.pdf?sfvrsn=382dec3c_2

Berger, W, & Foster, E (2020). *Beautiful Questions in the Classroom: Transforming Classrooms into Cultures of Curiosity and Inquiry.* USA: Corwin Publishers

Biggs, J, & Collis, KF (1981). *Evaluating the Quality of Learning: The SOLO Taxonomy.* New York: Academic Press

Boudett, KP, City, EA, & Murnane, RJ (2013). *Data Wise: A Step-by-Step Guide to Using Assessment Results to Improve Teaching and Learning.* USA: Harvard Educational Publishing Group

Breakspear, S, & Jones, BR (2020). *Teaching Sprints: How Overloaded Educators Can Keep Getting Better.* USA: Corwin Publishers

Broadfoot, PM, Daugherty, R, Gardner, J, Harlen, W, James, M, & Stobart, G (2002). *Assessment for Learning: 10 Principles.* Nuffield Foundation and University of Cambridge School of Education, Cambridge, UK

Carroll, A (2018, Feb 19). 'Video Feedback and Writing' [Facebook post]. Retrieved from www.facebook.com/groups/275176322846821/permalink/572508179780299

Cash, RM (2011). *Advancing Differentiation: Thinking and Learning for the 21st Century.* Free Spirit Publishing

Centre for Education Statistics and Evaluation (2020). *What works best: 2020 update*

Demore, W (2017). *Know Thyself: Using Student Self-Assessment to Increase Student Learning Outcomes* [Master's thesis]. University of Wyoming doi.org/10.15786/13686850.v3

Drabsch, T (2019). *NSW Curriculum Review.* NSW Parliamentary Research Service

Ellerton, P (2017). *On critical thinking and collaborative inquiry.* Education: Future Frontiers, NSW Department of Education

Fisher, D, & Frey, N (2013). *Gradual Release of Responsibility Instructional Framework.* International Reading Association. doi.10.1598/e-ssentials.8037

Fisher, D, & Frey, N (2021). *Better Learning Through Structured Teaching: A Framework for the Gradual Release of Responsibility* (3rd edition). Virginia: ASCD

Fisher, D, Frey, N, Almarode, J, Flories, K, & Nagel, D (2019). *PLC+ Better Decisions and Greater Impact by Design.* USA: Corwin

Fisher, D, Frey, N, & Hattie, J (2016). *Visible Learning for Literacy, K-12: Implementing the Practices That Work Best to Accelerate Student Learning.* USA: Corwin

Frey, N, Hattie, J, & Fisher, D (2018). *Developing Assessment-Capable Visible Learners.* USA: Corwin

Halpern, DF (2003). 'Thinking critically about creative thinking' in Runco, MA (Ed), *Critical creative processes,* pp 189-207. Hampton Press

Hattie, J (2012). *Visible learning for teachers: Maximizing impact on learning.* USA: Routledge

Hattie, J, & Donoghue, GM (2016). 'Learning strategies: a synthesis and conceptual model.' *NPJ Science of Learning,* 1, pp 1-13. doi.org/10.1038/npjscilearn.2016.13

Hattie, J, Fisher, D, Frey, N, Gojak, LM, Moore, SD, & Mellman, W (2016). *Visible Learning for Mathematics, Grades K-12: What Works Best to Optimize Student Learning.* USA: Corwin

Heard J, Scoular, C, Duckworth, D, Ramalingam, D, & Teo, I (2020). *Critical Thinking: Definition and Structure.* Australian Council for Educational Research. Retrieved from research.acer.edu.au/ar_misc/38

Heard J, Scoular, C, Duckworth, D, Ramalingam, D, & Teo, I (2020). *Critical Thinking: Skill Development Framework.* Australian Council for Educational Research. Retrieved from research.acer.edu.au/ar_misc/41

Hook, P (2006). 'Designing for differentiation in inclusive classrooms.' HookED. Retrieved from pamhook.com/wiki/Designing_for_Differentiation

Hook, P (2011). 'SOLO Taxonomy.' HookED. Retrieved from pamhook.com/solo-taxonomy/

Hook, P, & Mills, J (2011). *SOLO Taxonomy: A Guide for Schools.* Essential Resources Educational Publishers, Invercargill: NZ

Hopkins, D, & Craig, W (2015). *Curiosity and Powerful Learning.* USA: McRel International.

Hughes, M (2015). 'Teaching thinking skills in schools.' ACER Teacher Magazine. Retrieved from www.teachermagazine.com.au/article/teaching-thinking-skills-in-schools

Klenowski, V (2009). 'Assessment for Learning revisited: an Asia-Pacific perspective.' *Assessment in Education: Principles, Policy & Practice,* Vol 16, pp 263-268. doi.org/10.1080/09695940903319646

Lamb, S, Maire, Q, & Doecke, E (2017). *Key Skills for the 21st Century: An Evidence-based review.* Education Future Frontiers: NSW Department of Education

MacKenzie, T, & Bathurst-Hunt, R (2019). *Inquiry mindset.* Elevate Books Edu

McGuinness, C (1999). *From Thinking Skills to Thinking Classrooms: a review and evaluation of approaches for developing pupils' thinking,* Research Report No. 115. Department for Education and Employment, Norwich, UK

McMillan, JH, & Heard, J (2008). *Student Self-Assessment: The Key to Stronger Student Motivation and Higher Achievement.* Educational Horizons, Vol 87, pp 40-49

Mertler, CA (2016). "Leading and Facilitating Educational Change Through Action Research Learning Communities". *Journal of Ethical Educational Leadership,* Vol 3 (3)

Murdoch, K (2015). *The Power of Inquiry.* Seastar Education

National Council for Curriculum and Assessment (2015) *Focus on Learning: Students Reflecting on Their Learning.* Retrieved from www.ncca.ie/media/1926/assessment-booklet-4_en.pdf

NSW Education Standards Authority (n.d.). 'Assessment for, as and of learning.' Retrieved from educationstandards.nsw.edu.au/wps/portal/nesa/k-10/understanding-the-curriculum/assessment/approaches

NSW Education Standards Authority (n.d.). 'Effective feedback.' Retrieved from educationstandards.nsw.edu.au/wps/portal/nesa/k-10/understanding-the-curriculum/assessment/effective-feedback

NSW Education Standards Authority (2018). *Australian Professional Standards for Teachers*. Retrieved from educationstandards.nsw.edu.au/wps/wcm/connect/9ba4a706-221f-413c-843b-d5f390c2109f/australian-professional-standards-teachers.pdf?MOD=AJPERES

NSW Education Standards Authority (2020). *NSW Government response to the NSW Curriculum Review final report*. NSW Curriculum Reform. Retrieved from: nswcurriculumreform.nesa.nsw.edu.au/pdfs/phase-3/homepage/NSW_Government_Response_to_the_NSW_Curriculum_Review.pdf

Organisation for Economic Co-operation and Development (2008). 'Learning in the 21st Century: Research, Innovation and Policy.' In the Centre for Educational Research and Innovation's Assessment for Learning: The *case for formative assessment*, pp 1–24. Retrieved from www.oecd.org/education/ceri/oecdceriinternationalconferencelearninginthe21stcenturyresearchinnovationandpolicy15-16may2008.htm

Paul, R, & Elder, L (2008). *The Nature and Functions of Critical and Creative Thinking*. The Foundation for Critical Thinking: Dillon Beach, CA

Ramalingam, D, Anderson, P, Duckworth, D, Scoular, C, & Heard, J (2020). *Creative Thinking: Definition and Structure*. Australian Council for Educational Research. Retrieved from research.acer.edu.au/ar_misc/43

Ramalingam, D, Anderson, P, Duckworth, D, Scoular, C, & Heard, J (2020). *Creative Thinking: Skill Development Framework*. Australian Council for Educational Research. Retrieved from research.acer.edu.au/ar_misc/40

Ritchhart, R (2015). *Creating Cultures of Thinking: The 8 Forces we Must Master to Truly Transform our Schools*. Jossey-Bass

Ritchhart, R, & Church, M (2020). *The Power of Making Thinking Visible: Practices to Engage and Empower All Learners*. John Wiley & Sons

Ritchhart, R, Church, M, & Morrison, K (2011). *Making Thinking Visible: How to Promote Engagement, Understanding, and Independence for All Learners*. John Wiley & Sons

Roberts, M (2013). *Geography Through Enquiry: Approaches to teaching and learning in the secondary school*. Sheffield: Geographical Association

Rosenshine, B (1995). 'Advances in Research on Instruction.' *The Journal of Educational Research*, Vol 88 (5), pp 262–268. doi.org/10.1080/00220671.1995.9941309

Rosenshine, B (2010). *Principles of instruction*. International Bureau of Education. Retrieved from www.ibe.unesco.org/fileadmin/user_upload/Publications/Educational_Practices/EdPractices_21.pdf

Rosenshine, B (2012). 'Principles of Instruction: Research-Based Strategies That All Teachers Should Know,' *American Educator*, AFT – American Federation of Teachers – A Union of Professionals. Retrieved from www.aft.org/sites/default/files/periodicals/Rosenshine.pdf

Sanders, S (2016). 'Critical and Creative Thinkers in Mathematics Classrooms.' *Journal of Student Engagement: Education Matter*, 6 [1], pp 19-27. ro.uow.edu.au/jseem/vol6/iss1/4

Sharratt, L (2019). *Clarity: What Matters Most in Learning, Teaching and Leading*, pp 119-148. Corwin Press: California, USA

Sherrington, T (2019). *Rosenshine's Principles in Action*. John Catt Educational Ltd

Stobaugh, R, & Love, SL (2021). 'Strategies to Bolster Critical Thinking through Literacy.' *The Florida Literacy Journal*, Vol 2 (1) pp 23-28

Teacher Takeaway Podcast (2022). S2, EP 10: End of Term Reflections [Blog Post]. Retrieved from teachertakeawaypodcast.weebly.com/shownotes/s2-ep-10-end-of-term-reflections

Timperley, H, Kaser, L, & Halbert, J (2014). *A framework for transforming learning in schools: Innovation and the spiral of inquiry*. Centre for Strategic Education. Victoria: Australia

Vigors, A (2018). 'Measuring Student Thinking.' Retrieved from thinkingpathwayz.weebly.com/blog/measuring-student-thinking

Vigors, A (2018). 'Visible Learning: Learning Intentions.' Retrieved from thinkingpathwayz.weebly.com/learning_intentions

Vigors, A (2018). 'Visible Learning: Success Criteria.' Retrieved from thinkingpathwayz.weebly.com/success-criteria

Vigors, A (2019). 'Give 3 Feedback Routine.' Retrieved from thinkingpathwayz.weebly.com/give3

Vigors, A (2019). 'Routines for Self-Reflection.' Retrieved from thinkingpathwayz.weebly.com/routinesselfreflection

Vigors, A (2019). 'The Art of Questioning.' Retrieved from thinkingpathwayz.weebly.com/artofquestioning

Vigors, A (2019). 'Thinking Routines: Phases of Development.' Retrieved from thinkingpathwayz.weebly.com/thinkingroutines

Wells, C (2015). 'The structure of observed learning outcomes (SOLO) taxonomy model: How effective is it?' *Journal of Initial Teacher Inquiry: contemporary teaching and learning issues*, Vol 1, pp 37-39. doi.org/10.26021/845

www.ingramcontent.com/pod-product-compliance
Lightning Source LLC
Chambersburg PA
CBHW070350120526
44590CB00014B/1072